♠♣♥♦

The Poker Mindset

Essential Attitudes for Poker Success

♠♣♥♦

By

Ian Taylor and Matthew Hilger

Dimat Enterprises, Inc.
www.InternetTexasHoldem.com

The Poker Mindset: Essential Attitudes for Poker Success
Copyright © 2007 by Ian Taylor and Matthew Hilger.
Published by Dimat Enterprises, Inc.

Cover Illustration: Per Arne Dahl
Book Design: Andrew and Eva Kuczynski

ISBN 0-9741502-3-1

Matthew Hilger is also the author of *Internet Texas Hold'em* and *Texas Hold'em Odds and Probabilities: Limit, No-Limit, and Tournament Strategies.*

iPad and iPhone owners!

Winning Poker Tournaments is now available as a free iPad app called Poker Coach Pro and as an iPhone app called *Holdem Pro*.

Our Apple apps provide self-paced replays of all the hands and commentary from the *Winning Poker Tournaments One Hand at a Time* series. You control the action while getting inside the minds of these top players as they dissect and explain every move and decision. The app is a great companion for the book itself, yet at the same time is more interactive and more engaging than a standard e-Book.

Search the Apple's AppStore for *Poker Coach Pro* or *Holdem Pro* and try it out with a few hands for free.

Dimat is now on Facebook!

For the latest news on Dimat publications and upcoming releases, join our Facebook page -- search for Dimat Poker Books.

About Dimat Enterprises, Inc.

Our Mission

To publish today's best poker books and grow the game we all love.

Our Pledge

To Our Customers: Dimat is committed to the publication of outstanding poker books that combine cutting-edge content and strategy with clear instruction from today's leading players.

To Our Authors: Dimat treats our authors with respect and professionalism, providing top-notch publishing services while offering some of the best royalty rates in the industry. Cover, paper quality, readability, and graphics are expertly handled to make your book shine.

Our Books

Texas Hold'em Odds and Probabilities: Limit, No-Limit, and Tournament Strategies, by Matthew Hilger, 2006

The Poker Mindset: Essential Attitudes for Poker Success, by Ian Taylor and Matthew Hilger, 2007

Winning Poker Tournaments One Hand at a Time: Volume I, by Eric "Rizen" Lynch, Jon "PearlJammer" Turner, and Jon "Apestyles" Van Fleet, June 2008

Internet Texas Hold'em New Expanded Edition, by Matthew Hilger, January 2009

Advanced Pot-Limit Omaha: Small Ball and Short-Handed Play, by Jeff Hwang, June 2009

The World Poker Travel Guide, by Tanya Peck, January 2010

Winning Poker Tournaments One Hand at a Time: Volume II, by Eric "Rizen" Lynch, Jon "PearlJammer" Turner, and Jon "Apestyles" Van Fleet, February 2010

Peak Performance Poker, by Travis Steffen, July 2010

Small Stakes No-Limit Hold'em, by Ed Miller, Matt Flynn, and Sunny Mehta, September 2010

Advanced Pot-Limit Omaha Volume II: LAG Play, by Jeff Hwang, September 2010

Advanced Pot-Limit Omaha Volume III: The Short-Handed Workbook, by Jeff Hwang, September 2010

The Math of Hold'em, by Collin Moshman and Douglas Zare, May 2011

Winning Poker Tournaments One Hand at a Time: Volume III, by Eric "Rizen" Lynch, Jon "PearlJammer" Turner, and Jon "Apestyles" Van Fleet, fall 2011

About Ian Taylor

Ian Taylor is a professional poker player and writer. His articles have appeared in a number of websites and publications, mainly focusing on poker psychology, variance, and emotional control. You can find Ian posting on a regular basis in the Forum discussion group at InternetTexasHoldem.com.

Ian received a degree in economics from the University of Warwick in 1999, completing a thesis on risk tolerance and gambling. He worked in the IT sector for a number of years before embarking on a professional poker career.

Ian lives in Essex, England, with his long-term girlfriend, Rebecca, and their pet cat. When not playing poker or writing, Ian enjoys football, soccer, and reading.

About Matthew Hilger

Matthew Hilger's interest in professional poker is three-fold: playing, writing, and managing poker content websites. His first two books, *Internet Texas Hold'em* and *Texas Hold'em Odds and Probabilities*, became best-selling poker books around the world.

Matthew received his bachelor's degree in Finance from the University of Georgia in 1989. He completed a master's degree in Finance at Georgia State University in 1991 as well as a master's degree in International Business from Thunderbird in 1996. Prior to embarking on a poker career, Matthew worked in various accounting, finance, and consulting positions.

Matthew cashed eight times at the World Series of Poker between 2004 and 2006, including one final table and a 33rd place finish in the main event. He also won the 2002 New Zealand Poker Championship.

Matthew currently lives in Atlanta, Georgia, with his wife, Diana, and two sons, Joshua and Zachary. Matthew's other interests outside of poker include composing on the piano and traveling.

Acknowledgements

Matthew and Ian would like to thank the following people:

First and foremost, Rebecca Churcher for continual support throughout the time we have been writing the book and also for some valuable initial editing.

John Baxter, Ammon Brown, Neil Dewhurst, Peter Field, Jane Griscti, Tony Pillinger, Erik Rand, and Tyler Zutz for proofreading, editing, and providing some valuable poker insights.

Rob Keller and Lisa Keller for checking the math and statistics.

Ed "Fasteddy" Nordling for conceptualizing the front cover, and Per Arne Dahl for the cover design and artwork.

Neil Myers and Julie Risinit for style and copy editing. Susan Myers for the cover copy.

All the members of the Forum at InternetTexasHoldem.com, who contribute to making it the best poker community on the web.

Table of Contents

Chapter 1

Introduction

There are dozens of poker books on the market that are designed to teach the technical aspects of the game. They discuss which hands to play, how to play them, and when to fold them. These books explain pot odds, deception, value betting, semi-bluffing, and a million other things. Many do a very good job.

However, most poker books pay only lip service to the more human elements of the game. Poker is a game played by people, not robots. People have feelings, drives, and emotions that may cause them to act in unpredictable and illogical ways.

This book picks up where the others leave off. We will *not* be discussing when to bet, raise, call, check, or fold, as important as these things are. Instead, we will focus on other important questions such as:

• What is the correct mental attitude for poker?
• How do you cope when you lose big pots or have a bad run?
• What is tilt and how can you avoid it?
• What other psychological factors might increase or decrease your chances of winning?

Poker authors like to market their book as the most important one you will ever read. We are more modest. We suggest that this is the *second* most important poker book you will ever read. The most important will be the one that teaches you correct technical play, because nothing can compensate for that. This book picks up from there and shows you how to maximize your edge and prevent the self-destructive tendencies that many players have.

The mental, emotional, and psychological aspects of poker are under-represented in poker literature but are extremely important. Every poker player loses money they shouldn't, not through lack of knowledge or understanding of the game but through poor attitude, weak mindsets, bad reactions, and woolly thinking. Even people who are very calm and controlled in their ordinary life can become emotional, illogical, or deluded at the poker table. Poker is a game in which you will face situations and be driven down thought paths different from those you experience in everyday life. In fact, playing poker optimally may require you to make plays that go completely against your instincts.

In this book we take a detailed look at the psychological side of poker. First, we outline the correct Poker Mindset with which to approach the game. The Poker Mindset sets the foundation and is a recurring theme throughout this book. Then we deal with the specific issues of losing big pots, handling downswings, and going on tilt. Once these foundations have been laid, we look at the importance of proper bankroll management, studying your opponents, and some additional, advanced topics. In the final chapter, we look at how poker affects the rest of your life and vice versa.

Who is this for?

Players of all abilities should benefit from this book, whether you are a complete beginner desperate to lose less money or a professional earning six figures per year through poker.

New players will gain knowledge and skills that most players have to learn the hard way. We outline some of the harsh realities of poker and give advice on how to deal with them.

Intermediate players will discover what may have been holding them back at the poker table, maybe allowing them to progress from a losing or break-even player into a winning one.

Advanced players will learn how to overcome some of the boundaries that have been limiting their earn rate. At the top levels of poker, most players have a solid grasp of the technical aspects of play. It is the players who are best able to master the human element of the game that will prosper.

You may notice a bias toward Hold'em over other forms of poker in the examples in this book. The reason for this is that Hold'em is currently the most popular form of poker and the game that most readers will readily understand. However, the concepts in this book apply equally to Stud, Omaha, or any other variant of poker. We simply use Hold'em hand examples to ensure that as many people as possible will understand the points being made.

One last note: We may at times use masculine pronouns (such as he, him, and his) when referring to players. This is purely for ease of reading and is not intended to indicate any bias against female poker players. In fact, one of the great things about poker is that it is a sport in which men and women can compete on equal terms, and in which both have the same potential to succeed.

Whether you are male or female, a beginner or an advanced player, young or old, we hope that *The Poker Mindset* will help you to improve your play. Read on to discover a whole new way of looking at the game.

Chapter 2

The Poker Mindset

"Victorious warriors win first and then go to war, while defeated warriors go to war first and then seek to win." – Sun Tzu
(from *The Art of War*)

Over time, successful poker players develop a repertoire of technical skills that they bring to the table. Such skills include reading hands, correct pre-flop play, bluffing/semi-bluffing and value betting. These skills maximize their chances of making the best decisions at the table. Similarly, successful players also benefit from developing the correct mindset — a psychological toolbox to complement their technical one.

This chapter will help you to achieve just that by describing such a toolbox. It will outline the Poker Mindset: seven attitudes that every poker player should try to master, regardless of their game, limits, or technical skill. They are realities you need to be aware of and attitudes you need to adopt in order to succeed at poker over the long term.

Just like technical skills, the Poker Mindset will help you make better decisions at the table. This won't always be as obvious as, for example, knowing when to fold to a raise on the turn, but it is designed to increase the money you make in the long run. In fact, in some situations it could be argued that defects in your Poker Mindset could lose you more money than defects in your technical game. It is a foolish player indeed who considers the psychology of the game unimportant.

In this chapter we examine the Poker Mindset in detail. The following sections will introduce each aspect of the Poker Mindset one by one, explaining why it is important and the pitfalls should you ignore it. They are arranged in a logical order, starting with the most fundamental.

2.1. Understand and Accept the Realities of Poker

What kind of game is poker exactly?

Some people compare poker to blackjack. Both are played in casinos for money and involve a mixture of luck and skill. Both benefit from a sound theoretical knowledge of the game, and successful play involves making the optimal play as often as possible.

Yet poker is nothing like blackjack. To start with, in poker you play against other players rather than the house, and your opponent plays by the same rules as you. Second, the strategic scope of poker is far larger. A person with a good memory could effectively become a perfect blackjack player with comparatively little study, whereas there is no such thing as a perfect poker player.

Some people compare poker to chess. Both involve deep strategy and require careful analysis for success. Both require you to outwit your opponent, taking both technical and human elements into account.

Yet poker is nothing like chess either. Chess is a game of perfect information. Both players know the exact state of play at all times, and there is little scope for deception or misrepresentation. Poker, on the other hand, is a game of partial information, with each player trying to discern what his or her opponents are holding. Chess also involves no luck, even in the short term. The outcome is entirely dependent on which player makes the best moves. In poker nothing is guaranteed in the short term. The luck element dictates that even over a reasonable number of hands, you can play well and lose, or indeed play badly and win.

The key to understanding poker is to recognize the ways that it is like chess, the ways that it is like blackjack, and the ways it is really like neither. Many players fail to achieve success in poker because they fundamentally misunderstand the game. What follows is what every aspiring poker player needs to know. We call them the Five Realities of Poker. Everything else discussed in this book flows from these.

1. Poker is a game of both skill and luck.

A popular debate among the poker community is whether poker is a game of skill or luck. Each hand dealt is effectively a new start, so logically it would seem that the way to win would be to try to win each hand. But the winner of the hand is effectively determined at random. In any given hand, the cards you receive are random, the cards your opponent receives are random, and any community cards are also random. A skilled player cannot do anything to increase his chance of winning the hand other than getting his opponents to fold.[1]

However, look deeper and you reveal the hidden skill element. Poker is not about winning the most hands; it is about winning the most *money*. In fact, the way the game is structured makes it a bad idea to try to win every hand. Each hand has only one winner, so you are better off picking your spots and playing only the hands where you think you have an edge. A player who tries to win every hand will end up losing a lot of money in the process.

The net result of this is that the stronger players tend to win *fewer* hands but *more* money.[2] It is difficult to think of any other game in which the best players win the fewest games; this unique facet of poker often makes it look like a game of luck.

But there is also a considerable element of skill. At various points in a hand, players are asked to make betting decisions. They must analyze the clues available to them (such as their own hands, the community cards, and their opponents' betting), and then use their judgment to make the best betting decision. Where there is judgment, there is room for error, and where there is room for error, there is naturally a skill element.

---

[1] Incidentally, this is the reason why bluffing is often over-rated by beginners.

[2] In general this is true, but sometimes (usually in no-limit Hold'em) you will find successful players who play quite loose.

2. In the short term, luck is king.

Although poker is a game of both skill and luck, in the short term it can be very difficult to spot the skill element at all. To win a pot in poker you must either have the best hand at showdown or force all your opponents to fold. You can increase your chance of winning by forcing as many opponents to fold as possible before showdown, but once you get to the showdown, it is purely about who has the cards, not who has the most skill. There will be occasions when you can win pots by forcing all of your opponents to fold, but obviously this is only possible when none of your opponents have a good hand. In short, the outcome of an individual hand in poker is largely based on luck.

As discussed in the previous section, the skill in poker is to lose less with your losing hands and to win more with your winning hands, but even this is an imprecise science over the period of one hand. For example, let's say you are playing no-limit Hold'em and go all in with a strong hand like A-K against a weak hand like 7-2. The odds of the A-K being the best hand on the river are only about 2 to 1. While this is a sizable advantage, it by no means guarantees winning. It is quite possible to make good decisions in a hand and be punished for it, or, from another point of view, make bad decisions and be rewarded.

Even over the slightly longer term, things don't always run smoothly for the skilled player. A good player can run badly for quite some time through a combination of being dealt a run of poor cards, taking bad beats, or simply being outdrawn at a higher-than-average frequency. Each individual hand contains a large luck element. It is easy for these individual slices of luck to aggregate into either a very good or a very bad run for a player, even over a seemingly large number of hands.

To illustrate this, suppose you play for a week and have 100 flush draws. In Hold'em, a flush draw on the flop is approximately 2 to 1 to get there by the river, so you ought to hit about 33 flushes in those 100 hands. Suppose if you're running well that you'll hit 40, and if you're running badly, you'll only hit 25. Now also consider that the same applies to your opponents' flush draws. The short-term luck of you and your opponents combined can make a huge difference to your week. If you run badly, you'll win 33-25=8 fewer pots than you'd expect on average. If your opponents run well, they'll win 40-33=7 more pots than you'd expect on average. All that adds up to a total of 15 pots less than you ought to win on average. Fifteen pots add up to a lot of money.

And that's just talking about flush draws — simply one of the hundreds of random variables you deal with at the table. How many of your pocket pairs make sets? How many times does a hand like A-Q run into A-K? How often do you flop two pair only to have your opponent flop a better hand? It does not matter how well you play; these types of statistics will affect every poker player in the short run, clouding the underlying skill element.

3. In the long term, skill is king.

The good news for the winning player is that if you play long enough, luck will cease to be a factor. Mathematicians know this intuitively, but for those of us less mathematically inclined, imagine a coin being tossed. On any given coin toss, there is a 50% chance of heads and a 50% chance of tails. If you toss a coin ten times, you would expect there to be about five tails and five heads. The probabilities for any given number of heads are as follows (figures are approximate due to rounding).

Number of heads	Probability
0	0.1%
1	1%
2	4%
3	12%
4	20%
5	25%
6	20%
7	12%
8	4%
9	1%
10	0.1%

As we would expect, five is the most likely number, and four and six are also quite likely, but the chance of a more extreme result is still significant. There is approximately a 17% chance of tossing seven or more heads.

But what if we toss the coin 100 times? If we now calculate the chance of getting 70 or more heads (the same proportion as before), we find it is now only 0.004% (or one 250th of one percent). The more times you repeat a random event, the less likely it is that you will get an extreme result.

This mathematical theory, often called "the law of large numbers," has important consequences in poker. As you play more and more hands of poker, the chances of you being extremely lucky or extremely unlucky decrease. Play enough hands, and the luck factor is virtually eliminated, leaving skill alone to determine results.

Unfortunately, it can take a very long time for the effects of luck to be negated. We can say that after 100,000 hands a winning player will almost certainly turn a profit, but even this isn't certain, especially if he is only a very marginal winner. Almost certainly in these 100,000 hands, there will be periods of a 100, 1,000, or maybe even 10,000 hands when the player loses money, but these should be negated by similar periods when the player wins more than he would expect. The more hands you play, the less important luck is as a factor.[3]

4. Poker is a game of small edges.

A lot of money flows back and forth across a poker table. For example, a $20-$40 limit Hold'em game might have an average pot of around $250. With pots this size, you would expect the players who were winning to be making a lot of money. After all, every pot they win will net them more than most people make in a day!

However, poker does not quite work like that. While you may be winning $250 at a time, the short-term luck in poker means that the money will be going back and forth across the table, so even a good player will not win too much more than his fair share. Once you take into account the rake, even the best players are barely turning a profit when compared to the size of the average pot. For example, in limit Hold'em, a good player might make only one big bet per hour.[4] It might appear that a winning $20-$40 player is winning hundreds of dollars at a time, when in reality he is probably making only about $40 per hour. Put another way, a good limit player will take several hours on average to eke out a net profit equal to the size of an average pot.

All of this stems from the fact that winning poker players make money from their opponents' mistakes, which are generally small in nature. In poker, any hand can win, and it is rare to be betting when you have the absolute nuts. So even when opponents call bets that they

---

[3] Consequently, this is why top players prefer slower blind structures in tournaments. More luck is involved in tournaments when the blinds increase quickly, because fewer hands will be played before the blinds reach a critical level.

[4] Online players tend to measure win rate as big bets per 100 hands. Many online players consider a good win rate in limit cash games to be about two big bets per 100 hands (of course, "good" is a relative term).

shouldn't, they still have a chance to win, especially if they know a little about poker and are not likely to put money into the pot with horrendous odds. These little mistakes add up over time, allowing the better players to win, but they will never win as much as it might seem they should given the average size of the pot.

5. Poker is a game of high variance

This is the effective conclusion of all the Realities of Poker outlined previously. Poker is a game of luck and skill, but in the short term, luck is king, so short-term results will be extremely erratic. Combine this with the fact that the good player's edge is very small, and the result is that winning players will have almost as many losing sessions as winning ones! In fact, a winning player may have even more losing sessions than winning ones, if the player is prone to ending his session once he loses a certain amount.[5]

Think about the $20-$40 limit player described earlier who makes an average of $40 per hour. In a six-hour session, he could expect to make around $240, which is about the same size as an average pot! It is not hard to see how the result of one or two pots can turn a winning session into a losing session or vice versa. A few consecutive losing sessions, and suddenly you are on a downswing[6] while a string of winning sessions signals an upswing. It is only after you have played thousands and thousands of hands that you can look at the aggregate results from all these upswings and downswings and see the long-term trend.

One final note — look back to the title of this section: "Understand and *Accept* the Realities of Poker."

You need to understand the Five Realities of Poker, but more important you need to accept them. For example, there is no point in understanding the huge short-term luck element in poker but then complaining that you just dropped 40 big bets in a session.

---

[5] Setting "stop loss" limits for yourself is covered in chapter 9.
[6] Downswings are a key topic in this book. See chapter 5 for a complete discussion.

A good player understands the Realities of Poker and accepts them, with the knowledge that it is the very nature of the game that helps him to be successful.

Or to put it another way, if you don't like the rules, don't play the game.

2.2. Play for the Long Term

From the previous discussion, it should be easy to see that there is little point in playing poker with the expectation of making money in the short term. In the short term, pretty much anything can happen; bad players can win and good players can lose.

If you are looking to make money from poker, you need to play for the long term and accept the short-term risks.[7]

The second attitude of the Poker Mindset is to play for the long term. But what exactly do we mean by "playing for the long term"? First of all, it is important to note that we are not talking about playing differently. There is a "correct" way to play every hand; the way that, on average, will win you the most money.[8] Your aim should be to play every hand that way. In fact, you need to be mentally playing for the long term *because* concentrating on short-term results can leave you vulnerable to making plays that have a lower expected value. If you are playing for the long term, you will not really care about the results of one session, and especially not one hand. When you are playing for the long term, you are satisfied with making the plays that will make you a long-term winner regardless of your short-term results.

A player who puts too much emphasis on his short-term results will feel ecstatic after a good winning session and depressed after a losing one. He will also be prone to the following errors.

---

[7] The long term is not a defined period of time in poker, and is defined broadly as "the time it takes for luck to mostly even itself out." This can vary from game to game.

[8] This is also known as the play with the highest expected value.

Playing to get even

Players who focus on the short term will do anything possible to avoid a losing session. If they are stuck, they will be inclined to keep playing until they are at least even. This attitude can have catastrophic results.

First, they may continue to play when tired or bored, resulting in them not playing their best. Second, this attitude may cause them to go on tilt,[9] especially if they slip even further into the red, making them doubly depressed. Of course, once they are on tilt, this is likely to cause them to lose even more, and they become more determined to get at least some of it back. As you can see, the result is a rather dangerous and vicious circle.

Protecting a win

The reverse is also true. Short-term players love to record a winning session and will tend to over-value them. A popular saying among casual gamblers is "Quit while you're ahead," which comes in part from the depressing feeling of being ahead and then losing all your winnings again.

One of the worst possible scenarios for a short-term player is losing his winnings, even if he loses it playing good poker. He will tend to quit while he is ahead, even if he is in a very good game and is playing well.

Alternatively, a short-term player might do something that could be even worse. He might stay in the game but start to play very conservatively, turning down plays with positive expected value in order to make plays that give him the lowest chance of losing a large amount of money.

---

[9] See chapter 6.

Tilting

A player more concerned with results than with playing well is far more likely to go on tilt because he will be affected more when things go badly. See chapter 6 for a more in-depth discussion on the types and triggers of tilt.

Getting mad at bad players

A player concerned with short-term results will be very annoyed when he is beaten by a bad play made by one of his opponents. He considers the results of his individual sessions important, and so any time he loses a pot he thinks he should have won, especially a large one, it hurts. This may cause him to hold a grudge against the player who made the bad play and he might even begin to play hands he shouldn't when his nemesis is in the pot. Alternatively, he may berate the weak player, which is always a bad idea, as the bad player may leave the table or at least start playing better. A player mad at losing a pot from an opponent's bad play is at risk of playing badly himself trying to recuperate the money he lost on the pot.

Making rash changes to his game

By playing for the long term, you are acknowledging that you can lose money in the short term through no fault of your own. On the other hand, a player concerned with the short term will instinctively try to change things if results are not going his way. While it is a good idea to continually review your play and make changes accordingly, it is a bad idea to make changes on the basis of short-term results. Note that this is a common error among intermediate players. When they are experiencing a run of poor results, they will constantly tinker with their game in an attempt to improve their results, not understanding (or not accepting) that their losses are mainly due to short-term luck.

For example, once when moving up limits, Ian found AA to be an unprofitable hand after 6,000 hands at that new limit. This didn't mean that he was playing it incorrectly,[10] and naturally it didn't mean that AA was an unprofitable hand at that limit. It simply meant that Ian had a run of bad luck when dealt aces in the hole over that comparatively short period. Had he tried to change the way he played aces after that period, the long-term result would almost certainly have been negative.

> Action Point: Review the errors that players with a short-term focus might make. Note any that you have made in response to short-term results. Do you now see why they are poor responses? Resolve not to make the same mistakes again.

In summary, playing for the long term really is the *only* way to play poker successfully. Players fixated on short-term results generally suffer unwarranted mental anguish that can result in bad decision making at the table.

2.3. Emphasize Correct Decisions over Making Money

The big advantage of playing poker for the long term is that you can focus on the only thing that is important: making correct decisions. Every poker hand you play will present you with decisions. In limit Hold'em, you decide whether to fold, call, or raise at any given juncture. Other games may contain different decisions. In pot-limit or no-limit games, you must decide how much to bet or raise, while in some games such as lowball and 5-card draw, you must also make a decision on how many cards to discard and which ones.

---

[10] Although there is the possibility that he was on a subtle form of tilt and had started to play it badly after a while.

At this point, what we mean by "correct" play warrants some discussion. In his excellent book *The Theory of Poker*, author David Sklansky describes the following as "The Fundamental Theorem of Poker":

> Every time you play a hand differently from the way you would have played it if you could see all your opponents' cards, they gain; and every time you play your hand the same way as you would have played it if you could see all their cards, they lose. Conversely, every time opponents play their hands differently from the way they would have if they could see all your cards, you gain; and every time they play their hands the same way they would have played if they could see all your cards, you lose.

This theorem gives an excellent and succinct explanation of how money is won and lost in poker, but it should not be used to determine whether a particular decision was a mistake or not. The problem is that Sklansky's theorem assumes that you have perfect information. In reality, we almost never have perfect information, as our opponent's cards are hidden.[11] In fact, if we did have perfect information, poker wouldn't be much of a game at all.

When we talk about the "correct play" in this book, we mean the best play that you could reasonably be expected to make given the information you have available. Our definition focuses on the practical side of play rather than the theoretical. To illustrate the difference between the two, consider the following hand.

You are playing limit Hold'em and hold A♣ Q♣. A large pot develops, and by the river you are heads up with your opponent on a board of

A♦ J♣ 9♦ 8♣ 7♣

---

[11] There are a few exceptions to this, but they are rare. Opponents will sometimes accidentally expose their cards, giving you perfect information. You might also find a tell that is 100% accurate. For the most part poker is a game of incomplete information.

Your opponent bets into you. What do you do? You are holding an ace high flush while your opponent could have any number of hands inferior to yours, including a set, a straight, a smaller flush, or even two pair. The obvious play here is to raise, and against the vast majority of opponents, this is certainly the correct play based on the information you have available.

However, what if your opponent had T♣ 9♣? You are beaten by the straight flush and so the correct theoretical play by Sklansky's definition is to fold. You probably have no conceivable way of knowing he has the straight flush, and so a raise is considered correct for all practical purposes, and a fold would be terrible. You would almost certainly call at least, even against an opponent who you have never seen bet on the river without the absolute nuts.

So why should we emphasize making correct decisions over making money? After all, isn't the goal of poker to make money? The problem once again comes down to the dominance of luck in poker in the short term. There is no way to guarantee making money in the short term; there are simply too many unknowns and random variables. A good player can virtually guarantee making money in the long term, but he can only do this by making correct decisions. A correct decision may end up losing the player money, but consistently making correct decisions is the only way to ensure long-term profitability. Focusing on anything else is futile.

For example, let's say you are playing no-limit Hold'em and are dealt A-T off-suit in late position. A solid early-position player raises a standard amount, and it is folded around to you. You recognize that A-T off-suit is a marginal hand that plays badly against early position raises and so you correctly fold. The big blind calls, and the flop is A-T-9. After two blanks on the turn and river, the dust settles and the big blind with T-9 suited wins a large pot from the pre-flop raiser who had A-K. Had you not folded pre-flop, you would have won a very large pot.

This is the kind of hand that upsets some players because they are looking at the hand in isolation rather than as just a small incident in the vastness of their poker career. While their fold did indeed cost them money in this hand, it was the correct decision (by both our definition and the Sklansky definition) that in the long term will save them money. Simulations tell us that against A-K off-suit and T-9 suited, A-T off-suit will be the best hand at the river only about 15% of the time. Your fold effectively made you money because you couldn't possibly expect to make more money in the 15% of the time you win in this scenario than you lose in the other 85%.

It is the same principle for any decision in poker. If you make the correct decision, then the actual result of the hand is irrelevant. Inevitably, there will be times when you lose money as a result of making the right play, while inevitably other players may win money by making the wrong play. All you can do is console yourself with the knowledge that over time these players will lose their money, and if you keep playing well, you will be in the best position to win it. Don't worry about winning money; worry about making correct decisions, and let the money take care of itself.

Action Point: The next time you play, take measures to ensure you don't know how much money you have won or lost in a session. If you are a live player, arrange your chips in messy uncountable piles. If you play online, buy in for a strange amount and keep randomly adding other strange amounts to your stack. If you don't know how much you are winning or losing, you should be able to concentrate on simply making good decisions.

2.4. Desensitize Yourself to Money

"Scared money can't win."

It's a much-used poker cliché, but an extremely important concept. The point it is trying to make is that if you are playing poker with money that you are afraid to lose, then you are less likely to win because you will be prone to making sub-optimal decisions.

Remember, making the correct decision is making the choice that will earn you the most money in the long run. If you focus on trying not to lose money, you are no longer trying to make the correct decision. Your decisions will now be made within the confines of damage control and decreased variance. You are costing yourself money as soon as you start giving up hands with positive expectation in order to decrease your variance. Poker is a game of small edges, and giving up situations with positive expectation can be enough to turn a winning player into a losing player.

Hopefully you are smart enough not to sit down at the table with your entire bankroll or next month's rent money. However, you can be playing scared even when you are not risking it all. Two factors tend to contribute to how likely you are to play scared:

First, how strong is your bankroll?[12] Do you have insufficient money in reserve to absorb any downswings you might have? Have you been losing recently and are now past (or dangerously close to) the mark where your bankroll is no longer sufficient for the limit you are playing? Have you recently moved up a limit and so your bankroll is now much smaller in terms of big bets? If any of these are true, then you will be more prone than usual to play scared.

Second, what is your attitude to money? Are you generally risk averse? Does your fear of losing money override your desire to win it? Are you willing to accept lower value for lower variance? Do

---

[12] For a more in depth discussion of bankroll issues, see chapter 7.

you fear losing money despite being adequately bankrolled? If so, then you have a problem, as these are not good attributes in a poker player. If you are unable to take a risk-neutral[13] attitude to poker, then you would be better off either quitting the game or playing with a bankroll so large (or at limits so low) that the cash amounts concerned no longer mean anything to you.

Potentially, you could fall into a number of traps by playing scared:

Not protecting your hand properly

If you are scared of losing, you often will not bet your weak made hands enough, leaving yourself vulnerable to being outdrawn. You will try to lose less when you are outdrawn but with the penalty that you will get outdrawn more often.

Not value betting your good hands enough

Value betting is one of the most important skills in poker. It is a bet made that you hope will make money when your opponent calls with an inferior hand. Not value betting properly, because you are content to win a small pot rather than committing more money for a favorable return, is a huge leak. It is especially common on the river, where you no longer have the incentive to protect your hand.

Playing too tight

If you are scared of losing money, then you may be reluctant to enter the pot without a very good hand, even when the hand figures to make a small profit. You effectively miss out on small profitable opportunities, which add up over time.

---

[13] Risk neutrality is defined as an attitude where a dollar lost has exactly the same value to you as a dollar gained. See chapter 3 for a more detailed explanation.

Not calling enough in big bet poker

If you're playing scared, you will be unlikely to call a large bet in big bet (pot limit or no limit) poker without a very strong hand because of the possibility of losing a lot of money or even your entire stack in one go. If your opponents catch onto this, then they will start stealing pots from you at every opportunity.

Not bluffing enough

Bluffing is, for the most part, an overrated skill. Beginners tend to believe that bluffing is what poker is all about, when in fact playing solid poker and bluffing very little, if at all, is generally a far more prudent strategy at the lower limits. However, if you never or at least very rarely bluff, then you will become very predictable to observant players at the middle-to-high limits. If you are playing scared, then you will tend to avoid trying bluffs, as they tend to be low- percentage plays in limit games or high-risk plays in big bet games.

In general, you should prefer to be in a position where you are able to handle a large loss with merely a shrug of the shoulders. Some players are able to do this, but most can't. The best most of us can hope for is that we keep our losses in perspective, remembering that moderate losses are inevitable in the short term. The important thing is that you don't let fear of losing adversely affect your play.

Obviously, as you move through the limits, it gets harder and harder to take some of the cash amounts you can lose in stride. Most people can accept losing $80 in a $1-$2 game, as they spend this amount of money on entertainment all the time. But for most people, losing $1,600 at $20-$40 is a lot of money. This is equivalent to a couple of months' rent or maybe even a month's wages for some people.

You can't really teach someone how to be insensitive to money. This is something you have to learn by yourself. As previously stated, some people are just too risk averse by nature to ever be able to achieve this. Regardless, there are three things that will help you desensitize yourself to money.

Experience – The more you play, the more you will get used to the cash amounts involved and the less they will affect you.

Bankroll – That $1,600 loss looks smaller when your bankroll is $20,000.

Separation – If your poker bankroll is completely separate from the money you use for day-to-day living, then the money you win and lose seems less "real."[14]

In reality, you will probably need to adopt a combination of all three of these measures. This is something you will have to do to be able to consistently make the right play and avoid "playing scared."

It is not easy to desensitize yourself to money, and for the most part, it is a process that requires time. Always be sure to play within your risk-tolerance limit and bankroll. As you build a bankroll to try and move up limits, work on your risk-tolerance also. Remember, you are never required to move up limits if it is too uncomfortable for you to do so.

2.5. Leave Your Ego at the Door

Watch poker on TV, play in your local card room, or even play online, and you will be amazed at the number of poker players who have seemingly huge egos. You will see players boasting about their skills, berating the play of others, boasting about their jobs or salary, and taking the most innocuous action as a personal insult.

If you are serious about winning money, you should leave your ego at the door when you sit down to play poker. Your ego can lead you into all kinds of trouble at the poker table.

---

[14] See chapter 10 for a discussion of the concept of separation.

The major problem with bringing your ego to the table is that it may become a factor in your decision making. Remember that the goal in poker is to make the correct decision at the table, the one that will win you the most money on average. You introduce a new goal when you bring your ego to the table. You now want to make the most money you can while keeping your ego intact. This new goal might result in you making a different decision than you would have made otherwise, nearly always a worse one. In effect, your ego is eating into (or possibly even negating) your winnings.

Your ego may lead you into several traps at the table, the following eight being the most common:

1. You might call bets that you shouldn't.

Psychologically, folding is like surrendering, which is equated with defeat. In an ego-fueled game, folding can seem extremely unattractive, especially if the pot is big and especially if you think there is a chance you have the best hand. When contemplating calling a bet, the questions going through your mind should be things like:

What is the probability I am ahead?
If I am behind, what are the chances of drawing out?
Am I getting the correct pot odds to make the call?
What is the likelihood that my opponent is bluffing?

Undue influence from your ego may lead you to consider irrelevant factors and think irrelevant thoughts such as:

Will I look like a coward if I fold?
Will I look stupid if I fold and he shows a bluff?
I don't want to let him get one up on me!

The result is that you will often call when analysis and probabilities dictate you should fold.

2. You might allow a personal feud to cloud or override your judgment.

Poker is by nature a confrontational game. Every dollar you win comes out of the pocket of one of your opponents and vice-versa. It is only natural that conflicts arise and players start to hold a grudge against one or more of their opponents. This usually occurs when one player has lost a large sum of money to another player, especially if some or all of that was due to bad beats. The losing player wants to get the winner back, show him who's boss, or make him look bad.

The unfortunate result is that you might let a grudge lead you into bad decisions. You might go out of your way to play in pots with that player to try to win "your money" back, or even just to try to get one over on your nemesis. You may also be paying so much attention to one opponent that you are giving insufficient attention to the other players at the table.

3. You are likely to try too hard to get even.

Remember when we mentioned earlier that it is a bad idea to try to "get even" when you are stuck in a session? One of the reasons you might try to do this is because of ego. Nothing hurts a player's ego like leaving a game with less money than he sat down with. It can seem like an admission that the game has beaten him, and that he would have been better off not playing. In a live game especially, it can be a bad feeling to have to stand up in front of the other eight or nine players, shove what remains of your stack into a rack, and leave — an admission of defeat of sorts.

So some players don't. They will stubbornly keep playing in the hope that they can at least get back to even and salvage some pride. Unfortunately, their play may deteriorate as they try to make more and more speculative plays in order to get their money back, and their concentration falls as they get tired or bored. The more they lose, the more they will want to try to win at least some of their money back. It is a vicious circle that could have been avoided if their ego had allowed them to walk away after losing a comparatively small amount.

> Action Point: Set a fixed amount that would represent a moderate loss in the game you play. This might be 25 big bets for a limit player or two buy-ins for a no-limit player. The next few times you lose that amount at the table, stop playing. This achieves little from a poker perspective but will get you used to the idea of quitting while you are behind.

4. You might play in games you can't beat.

Poker is only profitable in the long term when you play against players who are worse than you. As the popular poker saying goes, even the 10th best player in the world will lose money in the long term if he insists on playing with the nine who are better.

Players with big egos do not like admitting that they are outclassed, even to themselves. As a result, they may play in games that they simply can't beat. In the same way, if a game they are playing in suddenly gets bad (due to the weak players leaving, for example), they will stick around convinced that they can still beat the game, even if a better game is available elsewhere.

5. You might make plays to impress your opponents.

Sometimes you will be tempted to make plays that look good even if they have little chance of working. For example, you might try a raise on the river as a bluff or a check-raise on the flop with a weak hand. That is not to say that these plays don't have their place, but you should only make them for the right reasons. Your ego is interfering with your decisions if you are making crazy plays that only work once in a blue moon so that you can slam your cards down and say "Gotcha!"

The reverse is also true. Sometimes players will be embarrassed when they misplay a hand or try something that doesn't work. To try to minimize their embarrassment, they will do everything not to have to show down their hand. This may include folding to bets they should call or even folding to no bet on the end. Some players go even further and are reluctant to bluff in the first place because they are afraid that it might look like a stupid play if they're caught. Embarrassment is the flip side of ego, and it also needs to be eliminated from your game. Besides, your bonehead play might have great advertising value!

6. You might not drop down a limit when you should.

One of the most humbling things a poker player will have to do is to drop down limits. It is something nearly all players hate to do because it is an indication of failure to beat the level you are at, at least in the short term. Nobody likes to play in a game that they consider beneath them, especially in a live casino where their peers may see them at that game and realize they are running bad.

The fact is that you *must* drop down limits when you are no longer bankrolled to play at higher limits. Otherwise, you might be risking your entire bankroll to pander to your ego. There should be no shame in making a move that will protect your bankroll and ensure your long-term profitability.

7. You could inadvertently give away information to your opponents.

You will repeatedly see players demonstrating their knowledge of the game at the poker table. Among other things, they will:

*   Discuss why they played a hand a certain way
*   Tell other players what they would have done differently
*   Berate other players for poor play

From a strategic perspective, there is no advantage in doing this. If your opponents are weak, then it doesn't pay to advertise yourself as the table predator. On the other hand, if your opponents are strong players, you would like them to view you as a weak player in the hope they play incorrectly against you as a result.

So why do players feel the need to demonstrate their knowledge? Part of it might be to fill the silence between hands and to be social, but a large proportion of it is ego. Subconsciously or otherwise, poker players want their fellow players to look up to them as a good player. Most think they are good players, and they want everyone else to think so, too, even if it affects their win rate in the long term.

If you give away information about how you play particular hands, then that is even worse! Do you want to broadcast to the better players at the table that you will lay down top pair to a raise on the turn, or that you will raise a flush draw on the flop? Unknown to them, players who bring their ego to the table may be giving their opponents the tools to beat them.

8. You might scare away players who you would rather stay.

Of course, the nasty end of this verbal posturing is when decent but egotistical players berate and belittle other players for what they perceive as bad play. This is not only unpleasant, but is also completely asinine from a poker point of view. Poor players should be nurtured and cherished. Poor players make poker profitable for winning players and less costly for average players. If you look at bad players as your "customers," it is easy to see that berating them is just not good business practice.

When players are chastised, it is quite common to see them simply leave the game. Weak players generally play the game for fun, and it is no longer fun when they are being publicly embarrassed and ridiculed. Obviously, it is a bad situation when a poor player leaves the table, because the average strength of your opponents increases, especially at the higher limits where weak players are harder to come by. However, this is the risk that some people take just to satisfy their ego.

Learning to suppress or at least control your ego will help you avoid these eight pitfalls. Possessing and even flaunting your ego will not preclude you from being a winning player, provided you don't let it influence your decisions. In fact, some quite well-known players are renowned for the size of their egos. However, for the cash game player especially, your ego may be eating into your win rate. You have probably not heard of many of the very best cash game players. They play in high-limit games in casinos and on the Internet, quietly winning huge amounts of money. If you spoke to one of these players, he would probably be very modest about his success and might even deny he wins at all. These players understand that their win rate is far more important than their ego.

If you want to emulate these players, you may need to start taking a very different approach to poker. Forget about what other players think of you, because it simply isn't important. Online players especially can be fairly secure in the knowledge that they will never meet their opponents except at the table. Use the effort you would put into bolstering your ego in more productive ventures.

- Focus on your own game and on making the best decisions rather than worrying about what your opponents think of you.
- If an opponent puts a bad beat on you, instead of trying to get even, make a note of how he played the hand and use that knowledge to your advantage later.
- If you are stuck for the session and are getting tired, leave and come back tomorrow. After all, does it really matter *when* you get even, provided you are a winner in the long run?
- Rather than discussing poker strategy at the table, listen to what other players have to say and learn how they think.

- Instead of berating players for bad play, encourage them and try to make their experience an enjoyable one so that they are inclined to play with you again.

Your ego is the enemy. Work on eliminating it just like any other deficiency in your game.

2.6. Remove All Emotion from Decisions

A recurring theme in this chapter has been eliminating what is irrelevant or dangerous from your thinking. In the previous section, we learned how many players wrongly consider factors such as their ego and image when making decisions. Prior to that, we discussed how playing scared can cause you to make less-than-optimal decisions. In fact, much of this book is about concentrating on what's important while eliminating what isn't from your decision making. Emotion is another important factor that should be eliminated from your decision making.

Many players let emotion affect their poker decisions, yet emotions should have no impact whatsoever on the decision-making process.

In some sports, emotion can be an advantage. For example, a football coach may try to motivate his players by stirring up emotions of anger, hatred, or team spirit, which may rouse them into working a bit harder or giving a bit extra. Poker is different from football and other similar sports in that there is very little that emotion can do to help a poker player. Emotions do not understand pot odds or how to put your opponent on a hand. They do not help your starting hand selection or your ability to get away from a second-best hand. Emotions will only cloud your judgment and divert your attention to things you should not be thinking about.

The negative effects emotions can have on your game are numerous, and every player is different. As such, it would be impossible to list every possible impact that every emotion could have on your game. However, here is a brief guide to the most common emotions experienced at the poker table and their likely effect on your game.

Anger

Anger is a dangerous emotion to experience at the poker table. A player who is angry tends to want to lash out, and at a poker table he may lash out with chips, making bets and raises that he shouldn't. He may also be prone to tipping over the edge if the slightest thing goes wrong, such as taking a bad beat or suffering a period of bad cards.

Frustration

Frustration is a frequent nemesis of the poker player, because of the huge number of frustrating incidents that occur during a poker game. Frustrated players tend to act rashly, losing the ability to think through decisions properly.

Misery

A depressed player is rarely in the right mindset to play poker. He believes the world is against him and will spot every facet of the game that reinforces this belief. He will likely assume the worst, and hence miss raises and fold winners more than he should.

Fear

Fear of losing the money in front of you has already been discussed in this chapter. A player may also fear the other players at the table, causing him to avoid confrontation and miss value bets or raises.

Happiness

An unduly happy player is not likely to have too many problems at the table, but he be prone to making decisions without due care and to overestimating his own chances.

Pity

Feeling pity for a particular opponent may cause you to soft play them or help them to play better, neither of which will do your bottom line any good.

Pride

Generally comes before a fall! For the damage that this emotion can cause, see the section on leaving your ego at the door.

Nervousness

Some players have a tendency to get nervous, especially in large tournaments or when moving up limits. If you are nervous, you may be unable to concentrate and follow thought paths to their conclusion. You may also be subconsciously giving off tells. For example, nervous players often shake when they are holding a big hand.

Action Point: Write down the emotions that you most often experience at the table and what usually triggers them. Simply recognizing these emotions and what causes them is halfway to conquering them. The next time you play, see if you can avoid the emotional responses that you usually have, or at least reduce their intensity.

Unfortunately, very few players can completely switch off their emotions. We just have to accept and adapt to this facet of our personalities. However, a poker player does have two defenses against his emotions:

1. Do not play when you are in an emotional state that may cause your play to suffer.
2. Acknowledge your emotions, but don't allow them to affect your decisions.

The former is obviously easier to do and is often the appropriate course of action to take, especially if you are in a particularly emotional state. However, we must not forget that emotions are ever present in our psyche. No matter when we sit at the table, we will be feeling *something*, even though the level of emotion may be quite trivial. Even if we sit down in complete serenity, poker is a game that generates emotion in itself, so we will probably not stay serene for long.

Therefore, it is important to master the second of these defenses: accepting emotion but not letting it affect our decisions. In fact, this is the essence of avoiding and overcoming tilt, a subject that we discuss in detail in chapter 6. Whenever you are making a decision at the table, you must try to make that decision based solely on the cards and on your read of your opponent.

2.7. Dedicate Yourself to a Continuous Cycle of Analysis and Improvement

The great thing about poker is that every strategic level you master unravels yet more layers. For example, the first thing most aspiring players learn is to play tight; they learn which pre-flop hands they should play and which they should fold. Once they learn some basic starting hand guidelines, they generally notice a huge improvement in their win rate. However, they then find out that they are playing too passively post-flop. They learn to play good, tight, aggressive poker and they improve again, maybe by being able to beat a higher limit or to achieve a better win rate in their current game.

Beyond that, they have several new horizons to master: pot odds, reading hands, deception, semi-bluffing, manipulating pot size, isolating, etc. For every new skill they successfully grasp, they become better players and improve their long-term win rate. For players who continue to analyze, study, learn, and improve, the sky is the limit. You will never reach a point where you know everything there is to know about poker; even the best players are still learning.

However, playing poker is very much like driving an old car up a steep hill. You will make steady progress as long you keep the gas pedal down. But once you let off the pedal, the car will come to a quick halt. Worse still, if you don't get it going again quickly, it will start going backwards down the hill.

You must continuously strive to improve your game. Even though you may only notice a slow, gradual improvement, it is important to keep that momentum going. As soon as you stop trying to improve, your game will stagnate and then regress, just as surely as the old car rolling back down the hill.

New poker players, if they are serious about the game, are often eager to learn and will process and absorb a lot of information very quickly. As a result, their game progresses in leaps and bounds for the first few months, and they observe consistent improvement after that. However, many get to the point where they lose the enthusiasm to learn. They start spending the time they used to spend studying poker by simply playing, or maybe they start spending it on the golf course. They rely on fewer and fewer information sources, until eventually their poker education is limited to a cursory look through a poker magazine while waiting for a table.

> Action Point: Think back to when you first started playing poker and try to remember how keen you were to learn. Are you less keen now when it comes to studying poker? If so, why?

There are many reasons why long-time players might become less keen on learning over time. Here are some of them:

Complacency

When players are new to the game and are losing, they have a strong incentive to improve. They want to be like the good players who are raking in the money. They hear that playing winning poker at the lower limits is not difficult, and see that with just a little effort they could be making money playing a game they enjoy.

However, if you fast-forward a few months, this same player may now have improved to the level where they are winning. They are beating the lower limits for a bet or two per hour and are happy to be doing that. While they would like to be able to beat the higher limits and make some serious money, they no longer have the burning desire to put in the effort to do so. They have other things they would rather spend their time doing now that they can "beat the game."

Illusions of mastery

Poker is a lot like speaking a foreign language fluently. Most people never become fluent to the point that a native person could not tell the difference. There are in fact many levels of fluency. The first level is being able to have a simple conversation with someone. Later, you might be able to have a more complex debate. You eventually learn slang and then technical words so that you have the ability to conduct business or teach a class. When learning a foreign language, you often tread along at a certain level and then leap to the next one. At the next level, you recognize and have a deeper understanding and appreciation of what "fluency" really means.

Poker works in the same way, but unfortunately some players have a very limited view of what being a good poker player entails. Once they get to a certain level, they believe they have mastered the game and no longer need to spend time learning. They might have improved to a point where they are making money because of the weaknesses of their opponents, but do not realize that they still have glaring weaknesses in their own game. Metaphorically, they believe they have mastered the language once they can ask directions to the post office.

A common pattern with players like this is that they repeatedly attempt to beat higher-limit games and they fail (which they attribute to bad luck). Eventually they either go bust trying to beat higher-limit games, or they give up and stick to bottom feeding;[15] or some of the more thoughtful ones might finally realize that their game needs work and begin a new regime of study.

Loss of enthusiasm

Most people have a huge enthusiasm for the game when they first start playing. They want to spend all their free time playing and reading about poker. Eventually, though, the initial enthusiasm wears off, and while they still enjoy actually playing the game, the learning side of

---

[15] Bottom feeding is poker slang for playing in the lowest limits with the worst players possible.

the equation becomes less attractive. The result is a decline in the time spent analyzing results and studying the game.

Action Point: If you find yourself losing enthusiasm for the game, try learning a different type of poker. If you play cash games, try playing a few tournaments. If you only play Hold'em, spend a while learning Omaha. Variety is the spice of life!

Stagnation

Players will often find that their game has stopped improving, despite the fact that they are still studying hard. They will then lose sight of the link between study and improvement, and stop studying. Incidentally, this situation normally arises when players have been focusing on the wrong areas and using the wrong methods for study. Or maybe they are just having bad short-term luck and are not seeing good results for this reason. Either way, it is highly unlikely that they have reached a point where study will not help.

It is a big mistake to stop taking the time to improve your game. Poker is an extremely complex game, and the cycle of learning and improving should never end. One of the most popular sayings about Texas Hold'em expresses this idea clearly:

"It takes five minutes to learn and a lifetime to master."
– Mike Sexton

Top players may disagree on many things, but one thing that they will voice resounding agreement on is that they are still learning.

Some players have the attitude that once they reach a certain level, they are happy with their play and their win rate and have no real inclination to improve any further. What they don't quite understand is the concept of regression. Remember, with the old car on the hill, taking your foot off the pedal will not only result in you stopping but also in rolling backwards. In the same way, if a poker player stops learning, his play is likely to decline, at least in relative terms. The reason for this regression is two-fold:

First, you can pick up bad habits that you never correct if you stop studying the game. The long term in poker is so long that if you pick up a bad habit, it may take a *very* long time before you see it for what it is. For example, let's say you start playing K-J off-suit from early position in limit Hold'em. This isn't a major leak, but you certainly won't see top players recommending it. You may win a few pots both big and small and lose a few both big and small. Overall, you will not really know whether this is a winning play or not, since you are not studying your results.

Maybe this is only costing you 0.03 big bets every time you do it, but that adds up over time. You may be picking up other bad habits, too. Maybe you are folding on the river too often or not value betting your draws enough, or any number of other things that are not major leaks individually, but put together become a big problem. If you were analyzing results and reading articles and so on, you would recognize the mistakes and correct them; but as it is, without doing this, your game could go into free-fall.

Second, you will lose much of your ability to adapt to change. Although the rules of poker tend to change very rarely, the dynamics and strategies actually evolve quite quickly. While it's not likely that a good player will become a bad player overnight by playing the same game, there is a lot of new poker literature that provides new angles on old strategies and new ways of playing marginal hands.

You will be far less able to adapt to new challenges if you don't keep studying the game. For example, let's say your regular game gets a lot looser due to an influx of new, inexperienced players. The optimal strategies needed to beat these players may be considerably different from what you are used to. You may be unable to adapt if you have stopped studying. In real terms, your game has gotten worse.

In order to ensure long-term success at poker, you must commit to a long-term program of analysis and improvement.

So how should you go about it? The modern poker player has a number of tools available to improve his game, and you should use as many of these as possible.

Self-help – Take notes on the hands you are playing and study them in depth later. Remember to make notes on what players were involved in the hand and what you knew about them. Internet players can even get a transcript of their entire session by email so that they can study every single hand! In fact, this is a big reason for live players to try online poker — it is much easier to build a database of results to help evaluate your game.

Other players – Discuss poker concepts and strategy with other poker players whose opinions you trust. While a few good players are cagey about giving away their secrets, most will take the time to help a poker player who is looking to improve.

Books – Excellent books on poker strategy are available, no matter what your game or skill level. When you find a good book, read it several times until you thoroughly grasp the subject matter.

The Internet – The Internet is home to a vast array of poker-related websites, offering everything from quick tips to in-depth strategy articles. The Forum at our website, InternetTexasHoldem. com, is a great place to ask for help and receive the opinions of dozens of other players.

Of course, experience counts for something, too. Just make sure that it isn't the only tool you are using to improve.

Bringing It All Together

In this chapter, we have discussed seven important concepts that you need to take on board and understand.

1. Understand and Accept the Realities of Poker
2. Play for the Long Term
3. Emphasize Correct Decisions over Making Money
4. Desensitize Yourself to Money
5. Leave Your Ego at the Door
6. Remove All Emotion from Decisions
7. Dedicate Yourself to a Continuous Cycle of Analysis and Improvement

These are the building blocks upon which the rest of the book is based, so it is important that you understand all of these concepts in principle. If there are any you don't understand, go back and read the relevant section *now* before you move on.

Together, these concepts provide the Poker Mindset with which you should approach the game. Simply understanding the attitudes described in this chapter should help you make better decisions at the poker table. However, the rest of this book builds on these ideas and shows how they can be applied to a variety of situations.

Don't stop reading now, because we've only just begun!

Action Point: Identify which of these seven aspects of the Poker Mindset you have the most difficulty with. Go back and reread that section *now*. When reading the rest of this book, think about how it refers to the Poker Mindset (the book itself will refer to this term in the text many times). Pay special attention to those bits that resonate directly with the aspect you have identified as your weak point. This may lead you to identify and resolve other related weaknesses in your game.

2.8. Chapter Review

❑ The Poker Mindset consists of seven attitudes that you need to adopt in order to succeed at poker over the long term, giving you a psychological toolbox to complement your technical one.

❑ **2.1. Understand and Accept the Realities of Poker**
- You need to understand the Five Realities of Poker, but more important you need to *accept* them. The Five Realities of Poker are:
  1. Poker is a game of both skill and luck.
  2. In the short term, luck is king.
  3. In the long term, skill is king.
  4. Poker is a game of small edges.
  5. Poker is a game of high variance.

❑ **2.2. Play for the Long Term**
- If you are looking to make money from poker, you need to play for the long term and accept the short-term risks.
- A player who puts too much emphasis on his short-term results will be prone to the following errors:
  - Playing to get even
  - Protecting a win
  - Tilting
  - Getting mad at bad players
  - Making rash changes to his game

❑ **2.3. Emphasize Correct Decisions over Making Money**
- The big advantage of playing poker for the long term is that you can focus on the only thing that is important: making correct decisions.
- In this book a "correct play" is defined as the best play you could reasonably be expected to make given the information you have available.
- If you make correct decisions, your short-term results are irrelevant as you will make money in the long term.

❑ 2.4. Desensitize Yourself to Money

- It is difficult to make correct decisions at the table if you are scared to lose the money in front of you.
- You could fall into a number of traps by playing scared:
  - Not protecting your hand properly
  - Not value betting your good hands enough
  - Playing too tight
  - Not calling enough in big bet poker
  - Not bluffing enough
- Two factors tend to contribute to how likely you are to play scared:
  1. How strong is your bankroll?
  2. What is your attitude to money?

❑ 2.5. Leave Your Ego at the Door

- Your ego may lead you into several traps at the table, the following eight being the most common:
  1. You might call bets that you shouldn't.
  2. You might allow a personal feud to cloud or override your judgment.
  3. You are likely to try too hard to get even.
  4. You might play in games you can't beat.
  5. You might make plays to impress your opponents.
  6. You might not drop down a limit when you should.
  7. You could inadvertently give away information to your opponents.
  8. You might scare away players who you would rather stay.

❏ **2.6. Remove All Emotion from Decisions**

- Many players let emotion affect their poker decisions, yet emotions should have no impact whatsoever on the decision-making process.
- Emotions can cause you to make sub-optimal plays that you would not otherwise make.
- Many types of emotions can affect your game such as anger, frustration, misery, fear, happiness, pity, pride, and nervousness.
- A poker player has two defenses against his emotions:
  1. Do not play when you are in an emotional state that may cause your play to suffer.
  2. Acknowledge your emotions, but don't allow them to affect your decisions.

❏ **2.7. Dedicate Yourself to a Continuous Cycle of Analysis and Improvement**

- In order to ensure long-term success at poker, you must commit to an ongoing program of analysis and improvement.
- If you stop learning at poker, not only will you not improve, but your game is likely to regress.
- There are many reasons why long-time players might become less keen on learning over time, including:
  - Complacency
  - Illusions of mastery
  - Loss of enthusiasm
  - Stagnation
- Top players may disagree on many things, but one thing that they will voice resounding agreement on is that they are still learning.

Chapter 3

Overcoming Your Instincts

"It is impossible to overlook the extent to which civilization is built upon a renunciation of instinct." – Sigmund Freud

There are many different areas of the game to which we need to apply the Poker Mindset. The most important areas to confront are the ones in which we are naturally inclined to make the wrong decision. One reason that poor players are prone to making mistakes at the poker table is that many decisions in poker require assumptions or thought processes that are vastly different to those we require in our everyday life. In fact, many of the attitudes required to play good poker actually go *against* our instincts.

In order to understand poker, we need to identify those areas where we need to adopt slightly different thinking in order to get the best results. This chapter outlines six such areas, ending with what we will call The Six Truths of Poker Intuition. You will see not only how poker "changes the rules" somewhat, but also how the Poker Mindset relates to these changes.

3.1. Actions and Reactions

It is human nature to look for the link between an action and its result (the reaction). Making these links is the backbone of human learning. They can be on a very small and obvious scale, such as noting that when you stick a pin in a balloon, it bursts. Alternatively, they can be links made as a result of complex interaction, such as observing that when you get caught telling a lie, you are likely to be trusted less in the future. One of the keys to human development is to find and exploit as many of these links as possible. In fact, nearly everything we do on a day-to-day basis relies on previously observed actions and reactions.

One huge benefit of observing these reactions is that it allows us to make changes. If your action does not have the desired reaction, then next time you can change the action to see how the reaction differs. For example, if you throw a football to a friend and it goes over his head, the next time you will not throw it so hard. This may result in an over-compensation and now the ball hits the ground in front of him, so you make another adjustment and so on.

Such adjustments aren't necessarily scientific physical adjustments like the above. In the workplace, a team leader might introduce some new procedures to increase the productivity of his team. He will then observe any resulting changes and adjust his strategy in order to achieve the best result he can for the next period. Here the link between the action and the reaction is a little less obvious and will need careful interpretation.

When it comes to poker, the link between action and reaction (or in this case, between decisions and results) can be even more difficult to identify. Any given action can have a wide range of results, both favorable and unfavorable, and this makes the whole learning process a lot trickier. Applying the same methodology to learning poker as you would to learning to throw a football may cause problems.

Some scenarios in poker can be solved mathematically. For example, in limit Hold'em, it is easy to prove that it is almost always correct to call one bet with four cards to the nut flush on the flop. Most situations are far more complicated, though. You couldn't prove mathematically whether it is best to fold, call, or raise 66 from middle position, because there are just too many variables that are dependent on the precise situation. In these cases, you can either learn from others with more experience or simply rely on trial and error.

The problem with trial and error is that when we perform an action and the results are perceived as bad, we instinctively want to change the action in order to achieve a better result. This is a response of which the poker player must be very wary. When playing poker, optimal actions can yield negative results, while foolish actions can yield positive results. For example, we could raise AA pre-flop only to lose a lot of bets when an opponent flops a set. Alternatively, we might call a pre-flop raise with K-9 and bust an opponent holding A-K when the flop comes K-9-6. These are contrived examples, but the principle is the same for most decisions you make at the poker table.

Just because you are winning does not mean you are playing well, and just because you are losing does not mean you are playing badly.

This is a vital point for poker players to understand. Otherwise, you might end up making unwarranted changes to your game or continuing to make bad plays, on the basis of your short-term results. In the above examples, the player with AA might play too cautiously the next time he is dealt aces, and the player with K-9 will have reinforced his belief that calling a raise with K-9 is okay.

Action Point: Review the starting hand charts in a strategy book such as *Internet Texas Hold'em*. Do you play any hands not listed on these charts? The chances are that you play these hands because short-term results have led you to believe they are profitable. Whenever your own ideas of strategy conflict with the opinions of most other knowledgeable players, stop to consider the possibility that your opinion is based on a subjective hunch or a string of abnormal results.

Of course, it is imperative to learn from your mistakes so that you can improve your game. One of the ways of doing this is by analyzing your results. However, you can only begin to make changes based on these results when your analysis looks at long-term results, and the long term may be longer than you realize. As discussed in the previous chapter, it may take tens of thousands of hands for a player to even be able to approximate his long-term win rate. When looking at making certain plays, this number can be even higher because you may not get to make this play more than once every few hundred hands or more.

For example, let's say you are trying to determine whether it is better to raise with AA from early position or flat call in the hope of re-raising when it gets back to you. How much experimentation would you need to do in order to be reasonably confident that you are making the correct decision?

You are dealt AA once every 221 hands on average. Only about a third of these will be in early position (assuming a full table). Additionally, in some of these cases, an opponent will have already raised in front of you. So you will need about 700 hands on average just to make one test run. If you decide that 100 attempts of each play are a reasonable sample on which to base your conclusion, then you will need to play 140,000 hands!

One could argue that if it takes 140,000 hands to come to a meaningful conclusion, then the issue can't be that important anyway. But there are hundreds of scenarios in poker like this. If you are making changes to your play based on short-term results for all of them, cumulatively you may be giving up huge sums.

You need to understand that in poker, the laws of action and reaction do apply, but in a very different way than in everyday life. The results of your actions will be extremely volatile in the short term to the point where they are almost not worth worrying about. Most players have trouble grasping this and ask themselves questions like:

- How can I lose against players obviously playing worse than me?
- How can I win one night and then lose the following night playing equally well?
- Why don't I seem to be hitting any flushes/straights/sets lately?

The ability of online players to analyze playing statistics can lead them to ask deeper and more specific questions:

- Why do I lose overall with A-J when I win with both A-Q and A-T?
- Why is 8-4 suited a profitable hand for me?
- Why is this player a big winner when his statistics show he plays badly?

In any poker game, whether it is live or online, you will probably find players asking themselves questions similar to these. These players will tend to act irrationally on their observations. They will start playing 8-4 suited and get wary of A-J. They will give up their drawing hands too quickly and get frustrated by bad beats. In short, they will do a whole lot of things that will harm them in the long term.

Don't be one of these players; make sure that when you make a *definitive* link between a poker play and its results, you are looking at the result of many, many trials. One problem with this is that you are often faced with decisions where you only have limited information, such as the playing styles of new opponents. In these cases, be sure to understand that you are basing your decisions on inconclusive data, and be prepared to adjust your play as you gain more information. The problem is that many players have a selective memory and end up arriving at conclusions about the long term based on just a few hands where they had either good or bad luck. Concentrate instead on applying sound principles to your decisions rather than relying on what memory tells you may have worked or not worked in the past.

3.2. Setting Goals

Ambitious, driven people tend to set themselves goals in life. These can be long-term (such as raising a family or reaching a given level in their profession), medium-term (such as getting a promotion or getting their golf handicap down), or short-term (such as finishing a report on time or paying the bills).

Setting goals for yourself is generally considered to be a good thing because it allows you to focus on what is important and to measure your progress against the most important standards of all: your own. People without goals (either explicit or implicit) tend to be less focused and, some would argue, less likely to succeed.

In fact, there is little downside to setting yourself real-life goals. If you meet or exceed your goals, it gives you a great confidence boost and challenges you to set bigger, more-challenging goals. If you fail to achieve your goals, you will either be motivated to try that much harder or be forced to re-evaluate whether your goals were realistic. Either way, the fact that your progress is being measured can be enough to push you to greater results.

Following this logic, setting goals for your poker game must surely be advantageous. In fact, many players do set themselves goals at the poker table. These may be short-term goals, such as winning a certain amount of money in a session or doubling up in a tournament by a certain level, or targets to be achieved over the longer term, such as building their bankroll to a set figure by a certain date.

Unfortunately for these players, setting such goals is rarely useful, and in many cases can actually be detrimental to their game. Broadly speaking, setting poker goals for yourself can be good, but they should never be monetary targets. There are three important reasons why:

1. You have limited power to achieve monetary goals.

The whole point of setting goals in your career and personal life is to give you focus, as opposed to just wasting your time or pursuing other less-rewarding goals. Implied in this is that you have the power to achieve these goals, or at least the power to give yourself a better shot at achieving them.

What monetary goals do you have the power to achieve when playing poker? While you ultimately have the power to determine how much money you win (through playing well), it is completely pointless to set this as a short-term goal. First, you only have the power to significantly affect your results in the long-term, and second, you should be playing the best game you are capable of anyway.

2. Conclusions are difficult to draw when you miss a monetary target.

If you do miss a monetary target, then how will you react? One of the ideas of setting a target is that if you fail, you can find solutions to do better. If you miss a monetary target at the poker table, then what can you do? There is very little you will be able to draw from this failure in order to improve your game in the future. All you are going to get from this failure is disappointment.

If you fail to fulfill your own expectations or goals at the poker table, then you will certainly want to analyze your game. The problem is that there is always the possibility that your poor results were merely due to short-term luck. You may not have been playing any worse than usual or may even have been playing better.

3. Monetary targets detract from your true goal.

The most important reason to be wary of setting monetary goals at the poker table is that it can detract from your primary aim of making correct decisions. Remember that the Poker Mindset emphasizes correct decisions over making money. If you set monetary targets, then it may lead to situations where you are tempted to make a less-than-optimal decision in order to achieve your target.

For example, let's say that you have a goal of making 30 big bets in a week. Toward the end of the final day of the week, you have only made 20 big bets. It might be tempting to play an extra hand or two, or chase a couple of borderline draws so that you can hit that target. Alternatively, if you have surpassed your goal, you may play extra conservatively to make sure you don't dip below your target.

What if your goal is to double up in a tournament by the end of level three? If midway through level three you are still approximately where you started, you may be trying to "force" a double up too much, going out of your way to play in big pots and chasing weak draws. The effect may only be slight, but any influence on your play that reduces the likelihood of making a correct decision is a bad influence. You should never compromise your game for the sake of hitting an arbitrary target.

So is setting goals worthwhile in poker? If so, what kinds of goals should you strive for? Setting goals in poker *is* important, but you should be very careful about what goals you set, making sure they fulfill two important criteria: First, you need to have the power to directly achieve the goal, and second, the goal must not conflict with or detract from your ultimate aim of making the best decision as often as possible. Learning and development goals are good because they can be fulfilled away from the table. Try setting yourself a goal such as:

- I will read one poker book every two months this year.
- I will post a hand example in a poker forum from every session I play this month.
- I will spend at least two hours per week reviewing hand examples.

These are goals that you have the power to achieve directly, that are easily measurable, and that will not cause you to compromise your game. If you really feel the need to set yourself a goal when you are actually at the table, then make it this:

During this session I will play the best poker I can, making as many good decisions as possible.

For the serious poker player, this is the best goal you can possibly set.

Action Point: Review any poker goals you have set. Do they pass the test of being achievable and measurable without potentially conflicting with your decision making at the table?

3.3. Is "Average" Acceptable?

Being average is nothing to be ashamed of. All it means is that if you sorted everyone in a given population according to how good they are at a particular task, then you would land roughly in the middle of the list. Very few people have the ability to excel at everything they do. Chances are you will have to accept being average at many things, and probably worse than average at some things, too.

In fact, Western society is geared toward the assumption that being average is fine. An average office worker will never get fired. An average doctor will still make a good living. An average fireman is still a valued public servant. In fact, in most professions being average is perfectly acceptable,[16] so much so that people are used to it. Many people are satisfied with mediocrity, and few have the drive to consistently aim for the top.

Average for a poker player is never acceptable. If you are an average poker player, then you are losing money. Logic might dictate that you should be breaking even, but this is not the case for a number of reasons.

The rake

The house charges a rake or charges you by the hour. This removes money from overall circulation and means that a player who would otherwise break even will actually be a long-term loser. For example, if the average rake is 0.25 big bets and the player wins 10% of the pots, he will pay 2.5 big bets per 100 hands in rake. Hence, an average player who would break even with no rake will in fact be losing 2.5 big bets per 100 hands.

Other costs

This one is mainly applicable to live players. If you break even playing poker, then effectively you will have "lost" any incidental costs associated with playing. These include gas to drive to the casino, tips for the dealer and the cocktail waitress, and any other additional costs you would not have otherwise incurred. Of course, most people don't count these costs when determining whether or not they are winning at poker (except dealer tips), but for a serious player they must be a consideration.

Good players play more

The problem with measuring an average player in median terms is that good winning players tend to play more, on average, than bad losing players. Even if you are better than 50% of players, you unfortunately are likely to be playing against more players who are in the top 50%

---

[16] There are a few exceptions such as professional athletes and actors. Generally, these are professions with very large pay disparities.

than those who are in the bottom 50%. Inevitably, this will result in you losing money overall, because you only make money in the long term by playing against opponents who make more mistakes than you do.

Delusion

If you think you are an average player, there is a good chance that you are actually below average. Most players tend to overestimate their own ability while underestimating that of others. This is a trait that you will observe in all areas of life, because most people tend to notice the weak points of others more than their own.

The end result of all of the above is that you will actually need to be far better than average to be a winning poker player. Poker is one endeavor where average is simply not good enough. If you want to make money at poker, you need to strive to be the best player at the table.

> Action Point: Develop a plan of action to improve your game. This should include setting aside time to study books, magazines, forums, and hand histories, and should be challenging enough to expand your horizons but not so demanding that you won't stick to it. It's time to step up from being an average player to join the poker elite.

3.4. Risk Aversion

Huge industries have emerged on the strength of the fact that most people dislike taking risks. The insurance industry is the most prolific of these, with the average person spending hundreds of dollars per year to protect himself against the possibility of a large financial loss.

Most people broadly accept the fact that they should insure themselves against certain losses, but what is the basis for this? Some answers can be found by studying a branch of economics that deals with attitude to risk. The basic theory is that people are either:

Risk Neutral: If you are risk neutral, then you believe in the absolute value of money. For a true risk-neutral person, having $20 is exactly as good as having a 50/50 chance of $30 or $10. He will accept any gamble with positive expectation and refuse one with negative expectation.

Risk Loving: A risk-loving person likes to gamble. He will always take any positive or neutral expectation gamble, and may also accept a gamble with negative expectation, depending on how far the odds are stacked against him and how risk loving he is.

Risk Averse: A risk-averse person does not like to gamble. He will never accept a gamble with negative or neutral expectation and may turn down a positive expectation gamble.

Of course, it's not quite as simple as that. How can we explain someone who pays for homeowner's insurance and also plays the lottery? What category would he fall into? Attitude toward risk is actually far more complicated than being risk loving, risk neutral, or risk averse.

First, there is a "fun" element of gambling that makes some people appear more risk loving than they really are. Even generally risk-averse people will accept negative expectation gambles if the fun they experience doing it outweighs the value that they lose. However, there is no "fun" involved in hoping your house doesn't burn down or hoping you don't lose your job, so the same people will continue to act risk aversely in these areas.

People also naturally tend to be risk averse when it comes to large amounts of money. This all comes down to the utility of money. As people accumulate more and more money, each additional dollar becomes less and less useful to them. This means that the real value of money becomes less when dealing with large gains and more when dealing with large losses. To take an extreme example, if you were offered a choice between receiving $1 million or having a 50/50 shot at

$2.1 million, it would be foolish for most people to choose the second option, even though it has the highest expected value.

> Action Point: Think about your own attitude toward risk. How high would the cash amount involved have to be for you to turn down a 50/50 gamble with the payout 5/4 in your favor?[17]

In general, people tend to act in a risk-averse manner. While they may be indifferent about risking small amounts of money, they will try to minimize the difference between what they could win and lose[18] when the potential for loss or gain is significant. Risk is considered the enemy, something to be avoided or reduced wherever possible.

A commonly held misconception is that poker players must be risk loving.   Many are, but not all.   A risk-averse person may play poker if:

1.   The enjoyment he gets from playing more than makes up for the money he might lose. He probably wouldn't see poker as gambling, but more as paying for entertainment; or

2.   He is a winning player and tolerates the risk for the amount of money he wins. Remember, even a risk-averse person may gamble if he has a big enough edge.

Poker players whom you meet in casinos and in online poker rooms are not all compulsive gamblers. Most in fact are ordinary people, playing part-time with money they can afford to lose. Most do all the things "normal" risk-averse people do such as take out homeowner's insurance, take out payment protection on loans, and purchase life insurance.

---

[17] 5/4 in your favor means that you get $5 when you win for every $4 you lose when you lose the bet. For example, win $100 but only lose $80, or you win $250 but only lose $200.

[18] Known as minimizing variance.

No matter what attitude a poker player has toward risk in his everyday life, he must adopt a risk-neutral attitude when sitting at the poker table. If you want to make money at poker, then you must make the play that will win you the most money on average as often as possible. There is no scope here for risk control. You will start to have problems if you are playing a poker hand (or worse still an entire session) thinking anything along the lines of:

I want to win a lot of money here, but I don't want to risk losing too much.

Remember that poker is a game of small edges. You are eroding that edge even further unless you make every decision on the basis of maximizing expectation. If you erode that edge too often, then you will no longer be a winning player. A player who tries to play poker in a risk-averse manner may be prone to the following:

Chasing opponents out of pots too often

Some players try to chase opponents out of pots by betting and raising because they are scared of being outdrawn, ignoring the fact that they would have a better expectation by allowing their opponent to make a bad call.

For example, let's say you are in a no-limit cash game. You hold a strong hand on the turn and you put your weak opponent on a draw. A good play would be to make a pot-sized bet if you think your opponent would call that amount with insufficient pot odds in the hope of hitting his draw. However, a risk-averse player might go all-in here, encouraging his opponent to make the correct play of folding. The risk-averse player prefers a guaranteed "sure thing" of the existing pot rather than taking a calculated gamble to win an even larger one.

Now, this isn't a strategy book as such, and so we don't want to delve too much into the ins and outs of the above hand. There may be situations where an all-in is correct, either because your opponent's draw is very good or because you suspect he may call even an all-in bet. For example, depending on the stack sizes, your opponent might have the correct pot odds to call even an all-in bet. If you suspect that he would call an all-in bet without the correct odds, then you would surely want to bet the maximum.

The point is that trying to protect your hand as much as possible is not always the best play. Nobody likes to lose a pot that they believe they could have won by betting more aggressively, but the risk of merely losing this pot should not be allowed to interfere with correct decision making. All that should matter when making the decision is mathematical expectation. It is better to win $60 90% of the time than $50 100% of the time, no matter how wretched you feel the other 10% of the time that you lose.

Not value betting enough

When holding a likely best but vulnerable hand, many players will choose not to bet or raise for fear of a bad card on a later street souring the situation. They will forgo putting money in with the "best of it" because, subconsciously or otherwise, they would rather forfeit extra money when they win a pot than lose extra when they lose a pot.

A common example is when a player has a big hand on the turn but knows his opponent has a lot of outs. For example, he holds the nut straight with heavy betting action and figures his opponent probably has a set. A risk-averse player might wait to see what the river brings before putting in too much money. That way, if the board pairs on the river (giving his opponent a full house), the risk-averse player can avoid losing too much money. However, from the perspective of maximizing positive expectation, you should be trying to win as many bets as possible when you hold the nuts.

Note that this is almost the opposite of the previous error, and goes to show how risk aversion can manifest itself in different ways for different people.

Playing in less-profitable games

By and large, the best poker games to play in are ones where there are a lot of loose players. Your opponents generally will make the most mistakes in these games and so your win rate will be higher. The only downside is you will get a lot of bad beats in loose games. Many players will play weak hands, trying to chase long-shot draws, and will naturally hit one every now and then.

Some players genuinely believe that these tables are harder to beat than tighter tables. They will cite poor arguments such as:

- Top pair never holds up
- You can't protect your hand
- Everyone calling makes each individual call "less bad" as they are giving each other better pot odds[19]

On the other hand, some players acknowledge that looser tables are more profitable in the long run, but still choose to play on tighter tables because they are risk averse. They would rather have smaller, more-frequent wins than the large wins and large losses you experience in very loose games. Effectively, they give up long-term value to decrease their variance or risk of a large loss[20].

If you are one of these players, you are probably underestimating the value you are giving up. It might be easier on a day-to-day basis not to have to deal with the swings of "no fold'em Hold'em", but in the long term you might be crippling your win rate. At the end of the year you will find that you have won a half, a third, or maybe even less than you would have won playing in the better games. In fact, you may not even be able to beat the tighter games. Once you take the rake into consideration, you have to be a very strong player just to turn a profit on a table full of tight players. Playing on these tables by choice can be a huge error caused by being risk averse.

---

[19] This phenomenon is sometimes referred to as "schooling."

[20] It is worth noting that it may actually have the opposite effect. If you decrease the mean and the variance of a random variable then it may well be that the chance of a large negative value is higher.

There are other examples of risk aversion playing a role at the table. Some players will not raise for value enough because they are too scared of a re-raise, or they may fold a long-shot draw where they actually have odds to call.[21] Any decision where a desire to avoid a loss is causing you to avoid a positive expectation play is a sign that you are bringing counter-productive risk aversion to the table.

For many players, risk aversion is directly linked to the limit they are playing. This goes back to what we were saying earlier about people being more risk averse when they stand to lose large amounts of money. For example, a player may be perfectly content dealing with the $500 losing sessions he sometimes experiences playing $5-$10, but may become extremely uncomfortable once he moves up to $10-$20 and has to deal with four-digit losing sessions, even if he is sufficiently bankrolled for that limit.

At this point, it is often prudent to take a step back and stay at the level where you are comfortable. Playing with scared money gets you nowhere, as stated in the Poker Mindset in the previous chapter. If you play at a level where you are not comfortable with the swings, then you run the risk of acting in a risk-averse manner, whether consciously or subconsciously. In chapter 7 we look more closely at moving up limits and the issues that can arise from it.

3.5. Greed

We live in a society that holds greed very much in contempt. Labeling an action or an individual as "greedy" generally has negative connotations intended to convey that someone is taking more of a resource than he needs.

Of course, "greed" can be a highly subjective term. What somebody "needs" is very much a matter of perspective. However, ingrained in Western culture is the idea that taking more of something that you already have in abundance is bad. It is even one of the seven deadly sins!

---

[21] Tight/Passive players or "rocks" are stereotypically prone to doing this.

When playing poker, you need to get rid of all pretenses that greed is a bad thing. Greed is not only acceptable when playing poker, it is *vital*. In fact, the Poker Mindset helps us with this — *Understand and Accept the Realities of Poker*. You need to squeeze as much money as you can out of any situation. Remember, poker is a game of small edges, so you can't afford to leave any bets out there. Go for them all and don't be apologetic about it.

"Greed is good. Greed is right. Greed works." – Gordon Gekko from the film *Wall Street*

Much of our disdain for greed is purely subconscious, and sometimes it will emerge at the poker table. For example, some players will check down large pots on the river, or may not raise with a hand very likely to be the winner. Their justification to themselves is "The pot is big enough already, no need to be greedy."

This line of thought has no real logic to it. The pot is never big enough, and if you think you have the best hand, you should bet and raise! It may be greedy in the classic sense of the word, but in poker there is no penalty for this behavior. Occasionally, certain players might dislike you as a result, but in reality you are bound to annoy this kind of player through playing good poker anyway. Incidentally, when playing online, this is rarely an issue. The anonymity of the Internet generally means that people will always act in their own interest anyway, betting and raising with impunity if they think they are ahead.

A similar observation can sometimes be made when a player is having a good session. Some people will quit after winning a fair amount of money because they don't want to be greedy by trying to win even more. They subconsciously think the penalty for greed might be that they lose all of their winnings. Of course, this is also illogical. You can't possibly think there is someone punishing you for your apparent greed. It is just a knee-jerk reaction to an ingrained doctrine that greed is bad.[22]

---

[22] For a longer discussion of the best time to quit a session, see chapter 9.

In fact, the concept of greed doesn't really have a place at the poker table at all. Poker is a game, and the object of the game is to win money. What some might label as "greed" is simply following the rules of the game. Winning the most money you can is the object of poker. If your opponents do not like it, they should be playing a different game.

3.6. Woolly Thinking

What is woolly thinking? Simply put, it is any line of thought that contains a logical flaw — any deduction that, when you break it down, does not make sense. Even people who are generally considered intelligent may have thought processes that sometimes lead to bad conclusions. Most people fall victim to woolly thinking far more often than they realize.

For example, you might see someone walk into a shop and buy a candy bar. He then opens the candy bar, but it falls out of its packaging and onto the floor. At this point, some people will pick it up and eat it anyway; good luck to them (this isn't a book about hygiene!).

For the rest, the rational thing to do would be to buy another candy bar. After all, if someone wanted a candy bar five minutes ago, chances are he *still* wants one. If it was worth the money five minutes ago, surely it is still worth the money now. The only reason not to buy another one is if you were so poor that you could not afford it.

Yet many people won't! They will curse, then shrug their shoulders and move on without buying another candy bar. Somehow the fact that they bought and dropped a candy bar has made them unwilling to buy another one. If you asked them about this, they generally wouldn't be able to give you a reasonable account of their actions; they just don't want to pay more money for something they believe they have already paid for. In reality, they are not buying another one because of stubbornness.

This is just one very narrow example of woolly thinking. As in the candy bar example, wooly thinking in everyday life does not usually result in catastrophe. Any kind of woolly thinking that has serious consequences is generally eliminated by necessity. The problem when playing poker is that *every* decision is important and *every* bit of woolly thinking will cost you money. Worst of all, you will probably not realize you are doing it and so will have no idea how much it is costing you.

The following is a non-exhaustive list of woolly thinking that is often brought to the poker table.

Considering irrelevant variables

Introducing irrelevant factors into the decision-making process will cause you to make bad decisions. Two such factors were introduced with the Poker Mindset: leaving your ego at the door and removing all emotion from decisions. Your ego is often a trigger for woolly thinking, and your emotions can certainly foster woolly thinking and cloud your judgment. Also, be careful not to let the results of hands you have played recently influence your decisions. Do not make a poker decision for any reason other than that it is the correct play in the specific situation.

Misunderstanding probability

A flawed understanding of probability can lead to incorrect conclusions about random events. An example is *The Gambler's Fallacy* whereby a player will consciously or sub-consciously believe that a random independent event is influenced by previous random events. For example, if he has hit three flush draws in a row, he may consider himself more (or less) likely to hit the next one.[23]

---

[23] For a good understanding of applying odds and probabilities in Hold'em, try Matthew's book, *Texas Hold'em Odds and Probabilities: Limit, No-Limit, and Tournament Strategies.*

Results-based thinking

Simply put, results-based thinking is judging a decision based on the outcome of that decision. In poker, a bad outcome can result from a good decision and vice-versa; results-based thinking can result in a biased evaluation of the decision. As discussed earlier, action and reaction are only tenuously linked in poker.

Spurious regression

Spurious regression is a statistical term that describes how two unrelated variables appear to be related. For example, you may notice that one dealer tends to deal you better cards than another, when in fact, the cards from both dealers are entirely random and you are merely noticing short-term statistical noise.

Acting on principle

There is no reason to act on principle at the poker table. For example, you will lose a lot of money by calling an aggressive player down with a weak hand just because "someone needs to look him up on principle." Always act to maximize your winnings, never for any other reason.

Superstition

Superstition is an irrational belief that an object, action, or circumstance not logically related to a course of events influences its outcome.[24] Superstition has no place at the poker table, yet you see it quite a lot. People have lucky hands, unlucky hands, and strange beliefs such that you should always fold your next hand after you give a bad beat to someone. Every time you do this you are giving up value. If you really believe that there are forces affecting your chances of winning outside the bounds of conventional probability, then you would probably be better off not playing poker.

---

[24] Courtesy of www.dictionary.com

These are really just examples of the woolly thinking that you may be bringing to the table. Some woolly thinking is in fact so off base that it does not even make sense to most people. Ian knows a person who refuses to play blackjack in casinos because the dealer can see his hand. He believes that this gives the dealer an advantage, even though the dealer has no decisions to make in blackjack and so cannot use this information.

Fortunately for this person, woolly thinking has led him to a good decision; playing blackjack is a losing proposition anyway. However, if you are thinking like this, it is just as likely to lead you to a bad decision. Good poker players learn to completely eliminate woolly thinking from their game.

As a fortunate by-product, many will eliminate it from their everyday life as well.

Action Point: At the end of the day, try to write down everything you did today that could be classified as woolly thinking. This should include anything you do that has no logical reason, including all things that fall into the categories above, plus anything else you identify. Be honest with yourself; you won't be tested on this and can throw the list away afterwards. Note that listing these things has in itself made you feel foolish for doing them. Repeat this experiment periodically, and you should not only slowly break some of these habits, but you should also more easily recognize them when you are at the poker table.

Summary

In this chapter we have looked at six areas in which the way we instinctively think (or are taught to think) will get us in trouble at the poker table. It is important that you break out of your pre-programmed thinking patterns and develop a new kind of intuition — poker intuition, if you like. These are the Six Truths of Poker Intuition:

1. Actions and reactions are only tenuously linked.
2. Setting short-term monetary goals is counter-productive.
3. Average is not an acceptable standard in poker.
4. Risk neutrality is the only acceptable attitude to risk.
5. Greed is good.
6. Clear logical thought is required.

This is not something you can correct overnight. It involves a gradual reprogramming of your instincts over a period of time. Not all players have problems with all six of these instincts. Some people aren't goal oriented anyway, or are naturally greedy, or are very self-motivated. The important thing is to identify those truths that are applicable to you and work on them.

The next three sections of the book address some of the major obstacles that you will encounter at the poker table, specifically the issues of losing big pots, downswings, and tilt. Most players do not act appropriately when faced with these inevitable situations at the table as their emotions get the best of them. This chapter has shown you how you can overcome your instincts so that you can move up to the next step, which is controlling your emotions. Once we conquer our emotions, we will have all the tools needed to apply the Poker Mindset on a consistent basis.

3.7. Chapter Review

❑ Many of the attitudes required to play good poker actually go *against* our instincts.

❑ **3.1. Actions and Reactions**
  • In poker, the link between action and reaction (or in this case, between decisions and results) can be difficult to identify.
  • Just because you are winning does not mean you are playing well, and just because you are losing does not mean you are playing badly.
  • In poker, the laws of action and reaction do apply, but in a very different way than in everyday life. The results of your actions will be extremely volatile in the short term to the point where they are almost not worth worrying about.
  • Make sure that when you make a link between a poker play and its results, you are looking at the result of many, many trials.

❑ **3.2. Setting Goals**
  • Broadly speaking, setting poker goals for yourself can be good, but they should never be monetary targets. There are three important reasons why:
    1. You have limited power to achieve monetary goals.
    2. Conclusions are difficult to draw when you miss a monetary target.
    3. Monetary targets detract from your true goal (making correct decisions).
  • Setting goals in poker *is* important, but they should fulfill two important criteria:
    1. You need to have the power to directly achieve the goal
    2. The goal must not conflict with or detract from your ultimate aim of making the best decision as often as possible.

❑ 3.3. Is "Average" Acceptable?
- If you average player at poker, then you are losing money. Poker is one endeavor where average is simply not good enough.

❑ 3.4. Risk Aversion
- No matter what attitude a poker player has toward risk in his everyday life, he must adopt a risk-neutral attitude when sitting at the poker table.
- A player who tries to play poker in a risk-averse manner may be prone to the following:
  - Chasing opponents out of pots too often
  - Not value betting enough
  - Playing in less-profitable games

❑ 3.5. Greed
- When playing poker, you need to get rid of all pretenses that greed is a bad thing. Greed is not only acceptable when playing poker, it is vital.

❑ 3.6. Woolly Thinking
- Woolly thinking is any line of thought that contains a logical flaw — any deduction that, when you break it down, does not make sense. The problem when playing poker is that *every* decision is important and *every* bit of woolly thinking will cost you money.
- Some types of woolly thinking in poker include:
  - Considering irrelevant variables
  - Misunderstanding probability
  - Results-based thinking
  - Spurious regression
  - Acting on principle
  - Superstition

❑ Summary

- It is important that you break out of your pre-programmed thinking patterns and develop a new kind of intuition that we call the Six Truths of Poker Intuition:

  1. Actions and reactions are only tenuously linked.
  2. Setting short-term monetary goals is counter-productive.
  3. Average is not an acceptable standard in poker.
  4. Risk neutrality is the only acceptable attitude to risk.
  5. Greed is good.
  6. Clear logical thought is required.

Chapter 4

Bad Beats and Losing Big Pots

"Nobody is always a winner, and anyone who says he is, is either a liar or doesn't play poker" – Amarillo Slim

So far in this book we have:

- Outlined a Poker Mindset that will teach you to approach poker in the correct way.
- Introduced the Six Truths of Poker Intuition, which explain some ways in which the best approach to poker can be fundamentally different than the right approach to most other things in life.

The rest of this book will show you how, when, and where to apply this knowledge, one area at a time. Much of it will be spent discussing the psychological impact of variance. Variance, in this context, means the fluctuations in short-term results as a consequence of the inherent randomness of the game. The logical place to start this discussion is by looking at the smallest measurable unit of results, which in poker is the result of one hand.

It is obvious that in any given poker hand you will either win or lose.[25] When you win a pot, the emotions usually generated are positive, such as happiness, relief, and pride. Generally, these emotions will not adversely affect your game. They have a positive effect on your game by giving you confidence, allowing you to think clearly, etc. There is

---

[25] Or of course, the pot might be split. Also, in "Hi-Lo" forms of poker there is the possibility of winning half or a quarter of the pot. This can potentially lead to situations where you win the hand but get back less money than you put in. For simplicity's sake, we will not be discussing these situations in this chapter.

always a possibility you might become overconfident, but the negative psychological impact of this on your game is minimal.

With many players in each hand and only one winner, losing is the norm rather than the exception. When you lose a pot, it is generally only the larger ones that will cause any kind of emotional discomfort for the average player. For example, hands where you fold pre-flop will not cause you much heartache because you haven't committed any chips to the pot (except for possibly a blind). You will lose little or no money on the majority of hands you play, unless you are a very loose player. The hands that have a big emotional impact are those where you lose a big pot.

In limit Hold'em, we would probably consider a big pot to be eight big bets or more. In no-limit Hold'em any pot over 30 times the big blind would be considered a big pot. It is losing these pots that is the subject of this chapter.

4.1. What Happens When You Lose a Big Pot?

The last bet is called, the cards are turned over, and the dealer pushes the pot to your opponent, a large pot that you figured you had a good chance of winning. Maybe your opponent had a legitimate draw that hit, maybe he hit an unlikely draw (or "sucked out"), or maybe he had you beaten all along and you just didn't know it. Whatever the reason, you are second best and as a result win nothing. This is where the misery begins.

Players get upset when they lose a big pot because the human psyche is fragile and is often unable to cope with events that it cannot predict. While most poker players acknowledge that they are gambling and know that losing pots is all part of the game, this does not make it any easier to accept when it actually happens.

Obviously there is the financial aspect. Poker is about winning money after all, and losing a large pot means losing money, as a fair chunk of that pot probably came from your own stack. If you are a strong player and are in a pot at showdown, generally it is because you think there is a good chance you hold the best hand.[26] You may already be mentally adding the money to your stack, happy at having won such a sizeable pot. To have the pot taken away from you at the eleventh hour can be a significant mental blow.

There are other reasons why losing a large pot hurts so much. For some players, losing is an uncomfortable reminder of the randomness of poker, especially if they lost the pot through no fault of their own. It's like a voice in your head saying, "You can make all the right moves, but it means nothing; you are a slave to randomness." This relates to what was discussed in the previous chapter about action and reaction. People like to feel they are in control and that their actions have a predictable result. Unfortunately, poker is the antithesis of control and predictability, and losing a big pot is a reminder of that.

How much losing a large pot affects you depends on several factors, including:

How big the pot is

Obviously, the larger the pot, the more you will want to win it, and the more disappointed you will be when you don't.

How good you felt your chances were of winning the pot

If you are merely calling down on the off chance your hand is good, you will probably not be too hurt when it isn't. On the other hand, if you are betting and raising, fairly sure that your hand is best, then it can be a big blow when your opponent reveals the winner.

---

[26] There are exceptions. Sometimes a pot is so large that you will call down on the off chance that your hand is good, knowing you have little chance of winning.

How you lost the pot

There is more than one way to lose a pot. You can lose to a bad beat, where your opponent chased a draw against the odds and hit. You can lose to one of your own errors, through not protecting your hand properly or not throwing away a clear loser. Or you can simply lose when the cards don't fall your way. Your reaction will depend partly on your perception of why you lost the pot.

How your session or recent results have been going

How you perceive losing large pots will vary greatly when put in the context of your session or recent results. Losing a series of large pots will often have a compounding effect on our emotions, each hurting a little more than the last. Or, more generally, the worse your session is going already, the more you will be affected by losing another big pot. This can also happen over multiple sessions. If you are on a downswing, you will be more emotionally fragile and more prone to reacting badly when losing big pots.

Whether it is in a tournament or cash game

In cash games the value of a lost pot is obvious, but in tournaments there are more intangible factors. Losing a big pot early in a tournament is generally pretty easy to accept. You are so far from cashing that you don't place much value on your chips at this stage anyhow. However, once you are deep into the tournament, then you start to look at the big prizes available for the top spots. Losing a big pot at this stage represents not only losing the chips you had in the pot but also diminishes your chances of winning the big prize.

How adequately bankrolled you are

If you have a large bankroll, then it is easier to put a lost pot in context. If you have a small bankroll, the direct consequence of each lost pot will be greater, and so naturally it will hurt more.[27]

Your attitude

Bringing the proper attitude to the table conditions you to cope with losing big pots. This is what this chapter is all about!

When you look at all of these factors combined, you can see why it is difficult for many players to tune out their emotions completely. You will be able to disregard most pots, but losing the big ones will most likely affect you deeply. Even the player who is a picture of discipline and calm on the outside may in fact be mentally crushed when his straight loses to a flush on the river.

Action Point: Every poker player has their favorite bad beat story. Think about yours and try to see why it hurt you so much. See if you can relate it to the seven factors listed above, and also make a note of anything else that made that hand particularly meaningful to you. By doing this you might start to identify some of your own vulnerabilities.

Fortunately, what is really important is not how much losing a big pot affects you emotionally, but how it affects your play. Emotions come and go, but steamed-off money is gone forever. The hand is in the past, best forgotten. If you can learn anything from it, then it needs to be filed away as useful information, but in every other sense you must act as if that hand never happened.

The penalty for allowing one hand-gone-wrong to affect your play can vary from slight to enormous. Beware of the following pitfalls that may snare a player who has recently lost a big pot.

---

[27] This is discussed in greater detail in chapter 7.

Berating your opponent

Unfortunately, one thing that players love to do after losing a big pot is to berate their opponent for their play, especially if the loss (or the extent of it) was because their opponent played their hand badly. As we discussed in chapter 2, this is a terrible idea from the point of view of your win rate. You want bad players to play badly. Think about it: Why get angry when players make mistakes? Would you actually prefer that they play great poker? It doesn't make sense to try to educate your opponents, or even worse, get them to leave the game. Additionally, think about the other players at your table. You are effectively giving them hints about how you think and play, which the good players will remember and use against you.

Playing the next hand badly

It is difficult to concentrate on the next hand if you are still fuming about the last. If you are not 100% focused when the next hand is dealt, you run the risk of playing it sloppily and missing something you would normally spot. This also applies to subsequent hands, albeit to a lesser extent.

Playing badly in similar situations in the future

People naturally tend to shy away from situations that have hurt them in the past. This is a good survival trait for the rest of your life but harmful at the poker table. For example, if you lose a big pot playing JJ and are then dealt JJ again while still in mourning, you are more likely to play it badly.

Tilt

Sometimes losing one pot can be a trigger for going on tilt. Tilt is a word that most poker players are familiar with, and to play on tilt basically means to play worse than usual in some way.[28] The effects of tilt can be so catastrophic that it is important to fully understand any stimulus that can trigger it, including losing big pots.

The best way to avoid these pitfalls is to approach the game in such a way that the results of individual hands do not hurt emotionally. The rest of this chapter will identify the correct way to respond to the loss of a big pot. We will then explain how to attain a state of mind where you will automatically have the correct response by utilizing the Poker Mindset. Finally, we will look at "bad beats," which deserve a section of their own.

4.2. Reaction to Losing a Big Pot

Some players tend to react very well to losing a big pot (and indeed other adversity in poker), while others tend to react badly. Experience helps in some regards. A seasoned pro with years of playing experience will tend to react better than a new player just getting used to the short-term swings. For most players, learning how to react well to hands that go badly is a journey that lasts a long time.

However, it is a mistake to think that this journey is linear or inevitable. Some experienced poker players still blow their top when they take a bad beat, while some beginners have an instinctive Zen-like calm in the aftermath of even the most horrific hand. In fact, it is more useful to think of the journey as a series of four stages, where each stage represents a better response (and a better underlying attitude) than the last.

---

[28] Tilt is discussed fully in chapter 6.

Stage 1 – Anger

A player at stage 1 sees only the monetary value of a pot that he loses. When he loses a big hand, his initial reaction is to be angry, in the same way that someone who has had his wallet stolen would be angry. One reason for this is that he links the money he is playing with to what he could buy with that money. If the player loses $50, he thinks about a meal at a restaurant. If he loses $200, he might think of a stereo. If he loses $2,000, he might think of the beach vacation he could have had.

This anger may be directed at a number of possible targets, depending on what happened in the hand. The most common target is the opponent. This is especially true if the player believes he lost the pot as a result of a bad play by his opponent. For example, the opponent hits an unlikely draw when the correct play would have been to fold.

Many players will be very verbal in their anger, chastising and belittling their opponent for their bad play. This is especially common when playing online, where there is usually no reprisal for a hateful outburst directed at another player.

If the pot was lost as a result of bad cards (for example, they flop a straight but lose to a full house), the player might look for another outlet for his anger. In bricks-and-mortar casinos, the dealer is often the unfortunate recipient. Online players might start to question the randomness of the card shuffler. More-diplomatic players may simply blame their bad luck on fate, the poker gods, or whatever deity they believe in.

Players at stage 1 are putting themselves in a situation where their play is likely to suffer whenever they lose a pot. They will often start "steaming," which is a state where the player tilts by playing too loosely and too aggressively. They may also want to get even with the opponent who beat them or to keep playing until they get back the money they have lost.

It is very difficult to be a successful player while at stage 1. You might be a good technical player, but this will rarely compensate for the money you will lose playing when angry.

Stage 2 – Frustration

Players at stage 2 have learned to remove the more destructive emotions from their reaction when they lose a big pot. Losing big pots will still be painful, but this pain manifests itself more as frustration than anger. Players at this stage will be frustrated at the randomness of poker. They will often think about the "if onlys" of the hand.

> If only the river had been a blank.
> If only my opponent had folded on the flop like he should have.
> If only I had protected my hand better on the flop.
> If only he hadn't been dealt A-K when I had A-Q.
> If only I hadn't hit my draw while drawing dead.

The problem for players at stage 2 is that they are still fixated on short-term results. This is not necessarily an ignorance thing. Many players stuck at stage 2 realize that the results of individual hands are not important; it's just that they haven't really embraced the fact. Remember the first attitude of the Poker Mindset? Frustrated players understand the realities of poker; they just haven't accepted them yet. They have still not fully removed themselves from thinking about the money that was in the pot. Unlike players at stage 1, rather than associate the loss of the pot to the loss of material things, they tend to think of the loss in terms of the impact it will have on the session or on their bankroll.

Sometimes strong players get stuck at stage two because they keep looking at pots lost in terms of their win rate. For example, if their win rate is one big bet per hour and they lose a pot worth ten big bets, they think, "That's ten hours of profit down the drain." They don't realize that their one-big-bet-per-hour win rate already takes into account the fact that they lose their fair share of big pots.

Undoubtedly you can be a successful player at stage 2, but your attitude will be hindering you. While you won't be as prone to steaming as stage 1 players, you may well make a number of bad plays through frustration, and you will be prone to tilt, especially the loose or passive kind. This is especially true when losing several big pots in a short period of time. To fulfill your potential, you will need to embrace the idea of playing for the long term and allow yourself to move to stage 3.

Stage 3 – Acceptance

Players at stage 3 understand and accept the realities of poker — the first part of the Poker Mindset. They understand that the game contains a lot of short-term luck, and as a result they are destined to lose big pots sometimes. If they are beaten by a poor player hitting a long-shot draw, they will tend not to react badly because they know that in the long run, they make money when their opponents chase unprofitable draws.

That is not to say stage 3 players are not sensitive to the results of pots. They will still be pleased when they win a big pot and displeased when they lose one. They have just learned to put short-term results in perspective and concentrate on what is important.

Players in the acceptance stage are far less likely to tilt than players at stage 1 or 2. They realize that their opponents' mistakes make them money even if they lose that individual hand. They might still be vulnerable to minor bouts of tilt after taking a particularly vicious beating, but this will usually be sub-conscious. They will never intentionally alter their play as a result of even the toughest hand.

Stage 3 is a good attitude toward losing big pots. At this stage you will have every opportunity to be a successful player, and indeed this is the attitude that most successful players eventually learn to adopt.

Stage 4 – Indifference

It takes an extremely disciplined player with remarkable self-control to reach stage 4, and very few players will get there. A player at stage 4 will not register any mental anguish from losing a big pot. Rather than feeling anger, frustration, or even acceptance of the hand, he will be focused entirely on how his opponents played and what can be learned from the hand. Whether he won or lost is an irrelevant detail.

Stage 4 players realize that the long term in poker is the only thing that matters. The result of one hand is irrelevant and not even worth thinking about. The only thing that matters in any one hand is whether they made the right decisions. If they did, then it was a good hand.

Players at stage 4 have the perfect attitude toward losing big pots. If they ever go on tilt, it will certainly not be because of short-term results. This gives them a huge advantage over players who are unable to adopt this attitude.

To further illustrate the difference between the stages, let's look at a limit hand example from the point of view of a representative player whom we will call Rick.

Rick is dealt A♦ K♥ in middle position. He open raises, the player on the button re-raises, and the big blind calls, as does Rick.

The flop is A♣ K♦ 8♠. The big blind checks, as does Rick. The button bets, the big blind calls, and Rick check-raises. Both opponents call.

The turn is the 9♣. The big blind checks, Rick bets, the button folds, and the big blind calls.

The river is the 6♣. The big blind now bets, Rick calls, and his opponent shows 7♦ 5♦ for a backdoor straight.

How will Rick respond to this hand? It all depends on what stage he is at.

<u>Stage 1</u> – I can't believe it! What was he thinking about calling all those bets? He had nothing the entire hand and lucked out. What an idiot! This always happens to me, it's so unfair! I'm going to do my best to get back at him and win my chips back.

<u>Stage 2</u> – What a bad beat! Losing an eleven big bet pot to a suckout like that really hurts. How can you win at this game when players call down with garbage and then hit? I know in the long term he will lose all his money, but I really needed that pot. That has put me in a real hole!

<u>Stage 3</u> – Ouch! Oh well, that's poker I suppose. If he keeps playing like that, I will take his money in the long term, so I just have to be patient. I'll make sure I remember that he is a calling station and play accordingly. I wonder if there was any way of winning that pot had I played differently.

<u>Stage 4</u> – Okay, I now know that the guy on the big blind will call down with pretty much anything, so I will take that into account from now on. I wonder what the button had. Maybe he had JJ or TT. It's worth knowing that he will make a continuation bet in that situation. Maybe I should have bet out on the flop in the hope that the button would have raised? That might have driven the big blind out, although I'm not sure I want to drive him out if he's willing to pay off all those bets with such a weak draw.

As you can see, Rick has two advantages when he is at stage 3 or 4. First, he accepts the result of the hand and so is less likely to go on tilt, and second, he is using his time more productively to think about the things that really matter. These are two good reasons why every player should want to move beyond the lower stages to reach these levels of thinking.

Action Point: Re-read the above and try to position yourself according to how you typically respond to losing big pots. Note that you might not be exactly in a specific stage. For example, you might be somewhere between stage 1 and stage 2. Look at the next stage up and identify the mental attitudes that separate you from that next stage. Try to develop your Poker Mindset so that you can reach that new stage. Come back to this book in a few months and see if you have gotten there.

4.3. Applying the Poker Mindset

Naturally, every serious player should want to be at stage 3 at the very least. Although the difference between each stage is merely a change in attitude, unfortunately it is not as simple as flicking a switch. You might know what the right attitude is, but how do you make sure that you can adopt this attitude when crunch time comes? A really hot-headed player could read and agree with the above section, but will still get mad when he loses a big pot for two reasons:

1. Emotions are difficult to control. Knowing the correct way of looking at a bad hand and being able to do it are two different things.
2. While he may understand that his response to losing a big pot needs to change, his entire approach to poker might be wrong and everything goes awry from there. He needs to go back to basics to resolve his attitude problems.

The first of these problems is a difficult one to fix. If you are naturally an emotional or angry person, the best you can hope to do is to slowly adjust your attitude over time. Through experience and repetition you can hopefully convince yourself that getting mad over losing a pot is pointless and counterproductive.

The second problem we can fix, though. In chapter 2 we defined the Poker Mindset. This is the key to changing your attitude toward many things, including losing big pots. Just to remind ourselves, here is the Poker Mindset, the seven mental traits key to poker success:

1. Understand and Accept the Realities of Poker
2. Play for the Long Term
3. Emphasize Correct Decisions over Making Money
4. Desensitize Yourself to Money
5. Leave Your Ego at the Door
6. Remove All Emotion from Decisions
7. Dedicate Yourself to a Continuous Cycle of Analysis and Improvement

If you don't understand what any of these mean, go back and read the relevant section of chapter 2. All of these traits will, in some way, help you cope better with losing a big pot and understanding them is the key to understanding much of the material in this book.

Understand and Accept the Realities of Poker

If you understand and accept the realities of poker, then you will accept that poker is a game of high variance and that, in the short term, luck dominates. You understand that you will lose big pots, so there is no point in getting mad when you do.

Play for the Long Term

If you are playing for the long term, then you realize that short-term results are unimportant. The results of individual sessions are virtually meaningless, and the results of individual hands certainly are. You do not need to worry about losing one big pot as you will reap the rewards eventually by playing good poker.

Emphasize Correct Decisions over Making Money

What you should be asking yourself at the end of every hand is not "Did I win the pot?" but "Did I play the hand correctly?" If you make better decisions than your opponents, ultimately the money is yours.

Desensitize Yourself to Money

If the money in front of you is important to you, then you will be more affected when you lose a big pot. By desensitizing yourself to money, you will be better equipped to shrug off the loss of a pot and move on to the next one.

Leave Your Ego at the Door

While this won't make losing a pot any easier to take, it will mean you are less likely to take it as a personal affront and go after the opponent responsible. A player playing without ego is far more likely to make a rational, sensible response to losing a big pot.

Remove All Emotion from Decisions

Again, this won't make a lost pot any easier to take, but it will mean you are less likely to respond badly. While the feeling you get from losing a big pot can be unpleasant, at least you can carry on playing secure in the knowledge that it won't affect your play.

Dedicate Yourself to a Continuous Cycle of Analysis and Improvement

If you are focused on improving your game, then you are more likely to look at what's important after a hand. In other words:

What does that hand teach me about my opponent's play?
Could I have played that hand better?

If you are focused on these important things, then you will have less time to focus on your own disappointment at losing the pot.

Effectively, if you learn and embrace the Poker Mindset, reacting well to losing a big pot should come naturally. In fact, getting angry or frustrated will seem silly. The importance of reacting well to losing pots cannot be underestimated. As we have already discussed, it will dramatically reduce your chances of going on tilt, and will allow you to continue to play your best game.

4.4. Bad Beats

Ideally, we would all like to be at stage 4, where we are indifferent to the results of individual hands. However, very few people manage to get there, and the rest of us need to cope with losing big pots as best we can. As stated earlier in the chapter, how players react to losing a big pot will partly depend on how they lost the pot. Broadly speaking, there are three ways you can lose a pot:

1. Bad Play – You made a mistake, which cost you the pot or caused you to lose more money than you should have.
2. Bad Cards – Neither you nor your opponent made any errors, but the cards didn't fall right for you.
3. Bad Beat – Your opponent got lucky to beat you with a hand he should have folded before most of the money went in.

Of these, losses through bad cards are generally the easiest to deal with. There is no way that you could have played the hand any better, and you are less likely to get angry at your opponent because they played correctly to beat you. While players do regularly get mad when losing a pot in this way (often cursing their bad luck), the effect is usually the least severe. You will remember the times that you have *won* hands in the same way that you lost this one.

Losing a pot through bad play is a trickier proposition. In many ways, these are the hands that you *should* be angry about. You should be annoyed with yourself for making that mistake and resolve to not make a similar mistake again. However, most players don't even realize when they lose pots due to bad play. If they had known it was a bad play, they would probably not have made it in the first place. In fact, when players do get mad at themselves for making a mistake, it is often a hindsight call and no mistake was actually made (for example, maybe they folded a very unlikely winner on the river).

Bad beats are a different story altogether. The average player gets angrier over bad beats than over any other kind of lost pot. The reasons for this are not necessarily logical, but they are at least understandable. For the most part, the reasons are a combination of the following:

Entitlement

Players with a strong hand will often (subconsciously or otherwise) believe they are entitled to the pot. Mentally they have already won it and have added it to their stack. At this stage, losing the pot through any means is going to be painful, but losing it to a bad beat will be especially difficult to accept. If an opponent wins with a legitimate draw, then it just means the player underestimated his pot equity;[29] but if he suffers a bad beat, then it seems almost as if the opponent stole money from him. The player will make accusations (verbal or mental) such as "That should have been my pot as you should have folded."

Rewarding Bad Play

For the myopic player, bad beats are seen to reward bad play. As discussed in chapter 3, people like to see the link between action and reaction, and when a bad play results in winning a big pot (and the other way around); it undermines their belief that they can win money by playing well. In some cases, players are known to make illogical conclusions based on a string of bad beats, such as "It is more difficult to win at tables with too many bad players."

---

[29] Pot equity is a common poker term used to describe the proportion of a pot the player can expect to win on average at showdown.

Directed Anger

Anger is often stronger when there is something for the anger to be directed at. Most players know deep down that feeling angry at the dealer, the cards, or the poker gods is not logical. An opponent who plays badly and takes down a pot is a far more appealing target.

Of course, none of the above reasons makes a whole lot of sense. As discussed in the previous sections, losing a big pot through any means is irrelevant in the long term. The only productive thoughts that can follow are:

What does that hand teach me about my opponent's play?
Could I have played that hand better?

Any other thoughts are unproductive and often harmful. The reason that bad beats are singled out in this chapter is not because they are worse than any other way of losing a pot, but because they are better! This may sound like a strange thing to say. It is doubtful that the average player who has just had his set beaten by a backdoor flush would be particularly comforted if he were told that a bad beat is the best way to lose a pot. When we break it down, bad beats are not only the best way to lose a big pot, but they are also good news for winning players full stop!

"Bad beats are a good poker player's best friend." – Matthew Hilger (2004)

To see why this is, we have to go back and look at how winning players make money at poker. The reason that winning players make money is that they make the best play most often or, to put it another way, they make fewer mistakes than other players. While short-term results are very volatile, you are guaranteed to make money in the long term if you make fewer mistakes than your opponents. In fact, if you are playing poker and making fewer mistakes than your opponent, then you are effectively making money, regardless of the results of the hand, a series of hands, or even the entire session. Let's say that again and paraphrase for emphasis:

If you are making fewer mistakes than your opponents at the poker table, then you are making money.[30]

Note there is no mention of actual results in that statement, because short-term results are simply not important. Let's have another look at the sample hand from earlier in the chapter. The "villain" in this hand made several mistakes in the hand, but we will focus on the turn. Imagine you are in the shoes of Rick. You hold A♦ K♥, and on the turn the board is:

A♣ K♦ 8♠ 9♣

You bet, the button folds, and the villain calls with what we now know to be 7♦ 5♦. The math is simple. If the river card is a six, then your opponent wins the hand; otherwise, you win. The pot contains eight big bets (if we assume a 0.75 big bet rake), and it costs him one big bet to call. He is getting 8:1 on a draw that is 10:1 to come in. If he hits, he can be sure of getting in an extra bet on the river given your hand. He is effectively paying 9:1 when he was 10:1 to win the hand.

The first thing to note is that his call on the turn was not nearly as bad as it first looked. Because of the particulars of this hand, he was actually getting very close to the correct odds.[31] If we assume the button didn't have a six in his hand (highly likely, given he re-raised pre-flop), then it's closer still. Of course, that doesn't mean the call was close to being correct from a "good poker" standpoint. He could not be sure that you would call on the end, nor could he be sure that all his outs were clean. However, mathematically speaking, he wasn't giving up much value with his decision on the turn.

The second thing to note is that *you want your opponent to call here.* If your opponent folds to your bet, you win the eight big bets in the pot 100% of the time. If he calls, you win nine big bets (assuming he

---

[30] This is an effective mantra, yet slightly inaccurate. For example, you may make few mistakes, but the mistakes are so large that they nullify the many smaller mistakes made by your opponent. If you want a strictly accurate mantra, try "If the total value of your mistakes is less than that of your opponents at the poker table, then you are making money."

[31] Note that this only applies to the call on the turn. The call on the flop was a lot worse!

folds on the end when he misses) 91% of the time and lose one big bet (your call on the river) the remaining 9% of the time. If you multiply these probabilities out, you will win 8.1 big bets on average, 0.1 big bets more than if he folds.

In other words, if you play this hand out a hundred times, you will win an extra ten big bets solely on the strength of your opponent calling here. Out of those hundred hands, your opponent will hit his draw sometimes, but it doesn't matter because the times he misses will more than make up for the times he hits.

In this particular hand, your opponent hit his draw. You shouldn't look at it like you lost the pot. In reality, you won 0.1 big bets from his call on the turn, and even more from the mistakes he made on the previous streets. If he keeps making those errors against you, then you will make money and he will lose it. The *last* thing you want to do is berate him for his mistake so he stops making these calls.

Of course, this is all tied into playing for the long term. As we have repeatedly stressed in this book, the results of one hand are meaningless. However, we should not only tolerate bad beats, we should be thankful for them! Next time you are beaten by an opponent chasing an obscure draw and hitting it, consider the following:

Bad play makes you money in the long term

As illustrated in the example above, every time your opponent makes a bad call against you, you make money, regardless of whether or not you actually win the hand. Over the course of thousands of hands, luck will cease to be a factor, and you will reap the rewards of playing good poker. In fact, bad play is the *only* thing that makes you money, so don't complain about it.

Action Point: One of the most common bad beat stories concerns a big pocket pair being cracked by a pair of random suited cards that should never have been in the pot. Carry out this experiment. Take a pack of cards and remove the two black aces and the ten and seven of spades (these are your two hands). Shuffle the remainder of the deck and deal out five cards representing the flop, the turn, and the river. Repeat this experiment several times and note down how often the T♠ 7♠ wins. Complete enough trials and you will eventually notice that the pocket aces win about 80% of the time.[32] Think about this.

Every time you have a big pocket pair and your opponent holds junk suited cards, you are about a 4:1 favorite. You want your opponent to put as much money as possible in the pot. You certainly don't want him to fold, because that decreases your positive expectation. Of course, the 20% of times when they beat you stick in your mind far longer than the 80% of the time when you are being given free money.

Bad beats keep bad players playing

If there were no such thing as bad beats, then bad players would hardly ever win. If bad players hardly ever won, then they would go broke too soon and quickly lose interest in the game. It is the idea that any hand can be a winner and that any player can win on his day that keeps many long-term losers coming back to the table again and again.

---

[32] Alternatively, you can run this scenario a million times using the poker odds calculator at www.InternetTexasHoldem.com.

Bad beats encourage bad play by rewarding it

Many players complain that bad beats reward bad play, and this is true. However, this is a good thing! Weak players like winning money, and when they make a decision that makes them money, they are more likely to make that decision again in the future. Remember our discussion about action and reaction? When bad players win a pot with a weak hand, their play is reinforced with the result of winning the hand. These players don't understand that their decision will cost them money in the long run. These players focus on the wins. They remember the time they hit their runner-runner flush to take down a big pot for far longer than they will remember all the times they missed and lost a bet or two. Every time you take a bad beat, remember that it has just reinforced your opponent's belief that he is playing correctly.

> Action Point: Do you have a lucky hand? Something like T-8 off-suit that seems to do well for you despite all poker books telling you that it is garbage? It is highly likely that you are a victim of short-term focus combined with a selective memory. Take a big step toward embracing the Poker Mindset and resolve to stop playing your lucky hand.

A good player will take more bad beats than he gives

Taking bad beats is a sign that you are playing well. When you are playing against weaker opposition, you will take far more bad beats than you will give out, because you will generally have the better hand when you elect to play. In fact, when you are dishing out a lot of bad beats and not getting any, *that* is the time to worry.

Bad beats are an integral part of the game

When you signed up to play poker, you realized hands were decided on the random turning of cards, right? Whenever you have a random element, you have luck, and wherever you have luck, you have bad luck. In the long term, bad beats happen no more or less often than they should, and without them the game would be extremely dull.

All in all, good players should like bad beats. Once again, bad beats are a good poker player's best friend! While you should learn to handle the loss of all big pots in the correct manner, you should actually be pleased with bad beats. Your opponent's bad play is the key to your success.

4.5. Chapter Review

❑ The hands that have a big emotional impact are those where you lose a big pot.

❑ **4.1. What Happens When You Lose a Big Pot?**
- How much losing a large pot affects you depends on several factors, including:
    - How big the pot is
    - How good you felt your chances were of winning the pot
    - How you lost the pot
    - How your session or recent results have been going
    - Whether it is in a tournament or cash game
    - How adequately bankrolled you are
    - Your attitude
- When you look at all of these factors combined, you can see why it is difficult for many players to tune out their emotions completely.
- Fortunately, what is really important is not how much losing a big pot affects you emotionally, but how it affects your play.

- Beware of the following pitfalls that may snare a player who has recently lost a big pot:
  - Berating your opponent
  - Playing the next hand badly
  - Playing badly in similar situations in the future
  - Tilt

❏ 4.2. Reaction to Losing a Big Pot

- There are four stages in how players react to losing a big pot:
  1. Anger
  2. Frustration
  3. Acceptance
  4. Indifference
- Each stage represents a better reaction than the last.
- Players at later stages will be better able to rationalize the loss of a big pot and not allow it to affect their play.

❏ 4.3. Applying the Poker Mindset

- A player might read and understand the four stages to losing a pot, but still be unable to consistently react in a way congruent with stages three or four. There are two main reasons for this:
  1. Emotions are difficult to control.
  2. His entire approach to poker might be wrong and everything goes awry from there.
- Understanding the seven attitudes of the Poker Mindset can help correct your approach to poker, which in turn will help you to respond better when you lose a big pot.
- Whenever you lose a big pot, rather than focusing on your emotions, focus on these two important questions:
  1. *What does that hand teach me about my opponent's play?*
  2. *Could I have played that hand better?*

❑ 4.4. Bad Beats

- Broadly speaking, there are three ways you can lose a pot:
  1. Bad Play
  2. Bad Cards
  3. Bad Beat
- The average player gets angrier over bad beats than over any other kind of lost pot. Some of the reasons for this include:
  - Entitlement - Players with a strong hand will often (subconsciously or otherwise) believe they are entitled to the pot.
  - Rewarding Bad Play - For the myopic player, bad beats are seen to reward bad play.
  - Directed Anger - Anger is often stronger when there is something for the anger to be directed at.
- Bad beats are the best way to a lose a pot as you make money in the long term when your opponents make mistakes:
  - Bad play makes you money in the long term
  - Bad beats keep bad players playing
  - Bad beats encourage bad play by rewarding it
  - A good player will take more bad beats than he gives
  - Bad beats are an integral part of the game
- Bad beats are a good poker player's best friend!

Chapter 5

Downswings

"Everybody will eventually run worse than they thought was possible. The difference between a winner and a loser is that the latter thinks they do not deserve it." – Craig Hartman

The importance of what we discussed in the previous chapter cannot be underestimated. The attitude required to cope with the loss of one pot is effectively the same attitude you need to cope with variance on a much larger scale. In this chapter we zoom out and look at the trickier issue of coping with large monetary downswings, expanding on the advice given in the previous chapter.

5.1. Running Badly

A downswing is a phrase poker players use to describe a period when they earn significantly less than their expected win rate over a number of sessions. It is very difficult to define a downswing any more specifically than that, for reasons that will become apparent later in the chapter. All players experience downswings at some point, and they can be extremely troubling times indeed.

In reality, we will discover that downswings really don't even exist from a theoretical perspective. They are a figment of the imagination of the player involved. But the poker community talks about them, they believe in them, and they assign properties to them. So even though downswings don't really exist, we will use the term in this book.

When poker players talk about downswings, they are normally referring to winning players (players whose long-term win rate is above zero) losing money for a sustained period. However, it is worth noting that downswings may hold a different meaning depending on the player. All of the following may also technically be considered downswings:

- A losing player losing at a faster rate than he would in the long term
- A break-even player losing money for a period
- A successful player winning less money than he would expect

In this chapter we focus mainly on the traditional kind of downswing, when a winning player is losing, as this is the scenario that is so difficult for many players to accept.

Zooming out

In the last chapter we talked about players losing large pots, which is something that happens all the time and is unavoidable. Now let's zoom out a little and look at the bigger picture. What effect will that pot have in the context of the entire session? For simplicity's sake, let's continue with the hand example from the previous chapter. If you can't remember the details of the hand, don't worry; the only important thing at this point is the result. You lost 4.5 big bets on this hand, and if the last card had not made your opponent's unlikely draw, you would have won 5.5 big bets.[33] Hence, if your opponent's draw had not come in, you would be 10 big bets better off.

These 10 big bets could have a significant impact on your bottom line at the end of the session. A significant win becomes a modest win, while a modest win becomes a break-even session or a small loss. A break-even session becomes a modest loss, while a modest loss becomes a significant loss.

---

[33] The final pot size was 11 big bets. 4.5 of these were yours anyway, and so you can't consider them "won." We will assume that if the river was a blank, the villain would have folded.

And this is just the effect of one hand. Over the course of a session you may play in a number of big pots. Lose just a few more than your fair share, and a winning session becomes a losing session. In fact, to put it in perspective, most losing sessions you have ever experienced would have been winning sessions if only two or three cards had fallen differently.

Action Point: Review your records and calculate what percentage of sessions you record a win. Are you surprised at how low this number is?

The results of any given session are mainly determined by a few lucky cards either for or against you. Because of this, a good player can expect to record approximately as many losing sessions as winning sessions. If you manage to record a win in 60% of your sessions, then you are probably doing very well. Something in the region of 55% is more realistic for most players.[34] Part of the problem for winning players is that they intrinsically believe they should be winning more than 55% of sessions. Their expectations are not aligned with the reality of poker.

In fact, it could be argued that having a higher proportion of winning sessions is not necessarily a good sign. While winning is obviously better than losing, too many winning sessions might be a sign that you are quitting too early when you are ahead. Maybe you record a small win and then quit playing to make sure you don't lose it again. As we will discuss in chapter 9, this is a sign that you are applying the wrong mindset at the table. The results of your individual sessions should not be this important to you.

Because losing sessions are so common, even for winning players, the chance of having clumps of them together is very real indeed. If you experience a losing session 45% of the time, the probabilities of having

---

[34] This will vary from game to game. Top no-limit Hold'em players, for example, tend to enjoy a higher proportion of winning sessions than the equivalent limit player. Also, players who play more hands per session tend to record a higher proportion of winning sessions.

n consecutive losing sessions purely through the laws of chance[35] are listed in the table below.

Consecutive losing sessions	Probability (%)	Odds (approx.)
1	45.00	11:9
2	20.25	4:1
3	9.11	10:1
4	4.10	24:1
5	1.85	53:1
6	0.83	120:1
7	0.37	270:1

In other words, if 55% of your sessions are winning ones, every time you sit down at the poker table, there is approximately a 1 in 54 chance that your next five sessions will all be losers, or a 1 in 271 chance that your next seven will be.

These chances seem quite small, but if you play poker regularly, they are not that small at all. To put it in perspective, if you play five sessions a week, in any given year you are quite likely to have a streak where you lose money for seven sessions in a row. You are bound to have multiple losing streaks of at least five sessions every year. Play less and the bad streaks will occur less often in nominal terms, but they will last longer.

And it gets worse. So far we have only discussed the likelihood of strings of consecutive losing sessions, but in reality, downswings aren't just strings of losing sessions. They are *periods* where we consistently lose money over a long period of time. If you have a winning session,

---

[35] As we will discuss later in the chapter, a player on a downswing becomes more likely to experience more losing sessions than normal, which will make these numbers even higher.

it doesn't help a lot if you then lose that much and more in the next session. Usually during a downswing you will have a few winning sessions, which are blips in an overall downward bankroll trend. All you will remember is the downward spiral your bankroll took during this period.

Action Point: You need a pen and paper and a coin for this one. Write the number 100 at the top of a piece of paper. Toss the coin several times. Every time you toss a head, take 9 away from the total and every time you toss a tail add 10 to the total. Toss the coin many times, keeping track of the total as you go. In the long term you would expect the total to increase, but because the expected increase is so small, you will observe long periods where your total appears to be going down. This is a neat illustration of how downswings work in poker.

Zooming back in

The high variance in poker makes it inevitable that you will suffer sustained losses from time to time. These will not be rare, freak occurrences, but something that most players have to put up with regularly. New players are often surprised by the seemingly ultra-conservative bankroll requirements recommended by experienced players. They don't realize that what seems like a large amount of money for the limit they are playing is quickly eroded by a string of bad sessions.

Some players might think there is nothing to worry about in a downswing as long as they have the proper bankroll. With a proper bankroll, you can just play right through a downswing, right? In theory at least, this is quite true. If you could always look at downswings retrospectively or from a third-person perspective, then it *is* simply a case of waiting for better results to come.

However, this is easier said than done when you actually find yourself in the middle of a downswing. When results are not going your way over a sustained period, poker can seem like a very cruel game indeed. The times when you were winning seem like a distant memory, and no matter what you do, your results will just not turn around for you.

In fact, coping with a downswing psychologically may be the most difficult thing to do as a poker player.

Many players lose far more than they need to, suffer unnecessary heartache, and even quit the game due to their inability to cope with a downswing. The purpose of this chapter is to discuss the best way of dealing with a downswing when it inevitably comes. We will delve into the mind of a player on a downswing, explore what he might be feeling, and discuss the best ways to cope with these feelings.

Before you know it, you will be back on course.

5.2. The Reality of Downswings

In order to correctly respond to a downswing, you first have to understand them. In the previous section we illustrated how bad outcomes of individual hands ultimately cause bad sessions, which then have a tendency to clump together and cause downswings.

In fact, if you look at it from a purely theoretical perspective, downswings do not really exist at all. They are merely a name given to an observed pattern in a random variable, in this case, an observed aggregate result caused by individual session results. Individual session results are in turn just an observed pattern derived from the results of individual hands. Or, to put it more simply, when you look at your results and think you see a downswing, all you are seeing is the individual results of a number of hands.

Think of downswings like the Big Dipper that can be seen on a clear night. The Big Dipper is merely an observed pattern in the random arrangement of stars. There is not a lot you can really say about it other than point out its location, because it doesn't really exist. It doesn't have a substance or any real properties in itself.

Downswings are effectively the same. They are not an entity in themselves, but an observed pattern in results. Consequently, you have to be careful when talking about downswings, lest you inadvertently assign them properties that they simply do not have. For example, the following are statements that are frequently heard from the mouths of poker players.

- I'm on a downswing, but I think it has bottomed out.
- I've lost 200 big bets now, so the results must turn around soon.
- I'm not due another downswing for a while.

Can you see what is wrong with each of these statements? They all rely on the assumption that downswings are actual entities in themselves with a fixed shape, size, or frequency. In reality, you could never say any of the above with any degree of certainty. Let's take a closer look at these statements:

"I'm on a downswing, but I think it has bottomed out."

Error – Assuming that downswings have a fixed shape.

What makes you think it has bottomed out? Just because you have had better results in your last couple of sessions doesn't make it any more likely that your subsequent sessions will be better, too. You might go back to losing big the next time you play, and the downswing might actually continue for a while longer.

"I've lost 200 big bets now, so the results must turn around soon."

Error – Assuming downswings have a fixed or maximum size.

Two hundred big bets is indeed quite a large downswing in limit Hold'em, but it is by no means as large as it can get. In fact, a downswing has no theoretical maximum size. Although a 400-big-bet downswing is quite unlikely for a winning player, if you are already down 200 big bets, then there is no reason at all that you are protected from dropping another 200 straight away. In fact, the chances of it happening are *exactly the same* as those of dropping the first 200, neither more nor less. You don't magically start getting better luck once you have lost a certain amount of money.

"I'm not due another downswing for a while."

Error – Assuming downswings have a fixed frequency.

There is no reason that a player who has just had a large downswing and recovered will not suffer another downswing immediately afterwards. In fact, this is entirely possible and is one of the most soul-destroying things that can befall a poker player. While it would be great to assume that once you have suffered a large downswing, you will have a period of good results, nothing is guaranteed. You are just as likely to start running badly again as at any other time.

All of these false statements have one major thing in common: They are all trying to define downswings in the present or future tense. They are trying to predict future events based on past results, which is impossible. Poker doesn't work like that. Every hand is effectively a fresh start and the cards have no memory. If you play a hand while on a downswing, all other factors being equal, you have an identical expectation on that hand as you would if you were on a big upswing.

Players conveniently forget this simple fact when they're on a downswing. Pessimistic players think that they are more likely to lose money because they are on a downswing. Optimists think that because they are on a downswing, they are "owed" some good results and so expect better-than-average luck. Both positions are illogical and dangerous.

Let's see what we *can* say about downswings.

Size

A downswing has no maximum size. You will often see posts on poker forums where an experienced player tries to define downswings with a statement like "In limit Hold'em, any downswing up to 250 big bets is normal; anything more than that must be due to bad play." However, making such a neat distinction between bad luck and bad play is completely wrong. It is possible for a winning poker player to suffer a 250 big bet downswing, only for it to continue for another 250 big bets. Bad luck and bad play are both likely to play a part, but it is impossible to quantify the effect of each factor with certainty.

What we can say about downswings is that the bigger they are, the more likely it is that factors other than sheer bad luck are playing a part. If you are a winning limit Hold'em player, you can expect to experience 100-big-bet downswings regularly, 200-big-bet downswings sometimes, and 300-big-bet downswings rarely; anything bigger than that is rather improbable but nevertheless possible. If a winning player claims that he regularly experiences 400-big-bet downswings, then it is far more likely that tilt is a factor, increasing the magnitude of his downswings.

Shape

Most players have preconceived ideas about the "shape" that downswings tend to take. The most common conception is that you have a period when results go badly, followed by a turnaround of fortune (maybe with a transition period when you break about even), and then results swing your way and your bankroll climbs back to its previous peak and beyond.

It is not hard to see why players think like this. Retrospectively, this is probably how their previous downswings looked to them. What they forget is that during that period, lots of things probably happened that didn't fit in with this pattern.

- The downswing probably contained some winning sessions (blips or "false dawns").
- The transition period was probably not so smooth or defined.
- The upswing probably contained some losing sessions as well.
- The upswing might have occurred much more quickly, or indeed much more slowly, than the downswing.

In fact, the shape of downswings is completely arbitrary as they are formed randomly. It is possible that you will lose a few sessions but then quickly snap out of it. Alternatively, you might mostly recover from a downswing and then slump right back down again. There is no way to predict what the result of your next session will be by looking for patterns, because those patterns exist only in your mind. Once you start believing that downswings take a particular pattern, you will start to see these patterns everywhere. You only set yourself up for a mental blow when reality fails to live up to your preconceived ideas.

Action Point: If you have them available, look back over your records to your last large downswing. Do you remember at the time feeling like the bad results would never end? Do you also see how arbitrary the session results look in hindsight? Try to remember this the next time you are on a downswing.

Frequency

The discussion of how often you should experience a downswing is really a nonsensical one. Downswings do not exist; they are just an observed pattern in random data. You can never say you are due a downswing or not due a downswing or even how many you should get in a given time period. All you can expect is that from now on, in the long term, you can expect to earn a sum of money in line with your long-term win rate.

In a perfect world, you would be able to completely ignore downswings, at least in the present tense. Unfortunately, the psychological pressure of running badly for a sustained period of time makes ignoring them difficult. A player who is running badly can't help but wonder how long his bad luck will last. Managing a large downswing is one of the most difficult things you will have to do as a poker player, and the penalty for failure can be losing your entire bankroll. The rest of this chapter focuses on how to cope with downswings and what pitfalls to avoid.

5.3. Common Bad Responses to Downswings

Downswings are bad enough as it is, but there are lots of things you can do to make matters a whole lot worse. While the initial downswing may have been caused by a run of bad luck or bad cards, its length and magnitude may increase if the player makes bad decisions or if his game starts to deteriorate.

This section identifies the most common bad responses to downswings. Some are self-destructive thought processes. Others are conscious decisions that seem like a good idea, but are in fact harmful or at best have no effect. Here is a summary of these bad responses:

- Losing confidence in your ability and game
- Making radical changes to your play
- Getting obsessed with your losses
- Trying to ride out the downswing
- Moving up a limit to recoup your losses

Some of these mistakes are elementary, some are more subtle. Let's look at each of these responses in more detail to see exactly why they are bad.

Losing confidence in your ability and game

Downswings can last for a long time, sometimes weeks or even months. When you are deep into a downswing, it is sometimes difficult to remember what it was like when times were good. In contrast, when you are on a rush at poker, winning seems like the most natural thing in the world. You don't think that you're "getting lucky" as such; it just seems like you are making all the right moves and they are paying off. On the other hand, when you are on a downswing, losing feels like the most natural thing in the world. For example, you raise with A-K pre-flop because you know you should, but you don't expect to flop anything. And when you do flop top pair, you expect that you will be outdrawn. Seeds of doubt start creeping in:

> Am I playing as well as I was?
> Has the game gotten harder?
> Was I ever a winning player?
> Are the opponents who I thought were weak actually outplaying me?

While you are on a downswing, all of the above will probably go through your mind at one time or other. The problem isn't that these are bad thoughts to have. In fact, all of the above are valid questions that poker players should be asking themselves periodically. The problem when you are on a downswing is that these thoughts can take over. You ask these questions too frequently, and unfortunately often arrive at the wrong answer. Metaphorically, you start seeing monsters under the bed.

Bad conclusions lead to bad attitudes and ultimately bad decisions. Once you go into the game expecting to lose, this can be a self-fulfilling prophecy. You might change your game unnecessarily (see the next section) or subconsciously try to restrict your losses rather than maximize your winnings. Some players even quit poker completely because they think they can no longer beat the game.

While you will almost certainly need to assess your play objectively and make improvements during a downswing,[36] you must still maintain confidence in yourself and your overall game if you want to pull out of it and return to the good times.

Making radical changes to your play

A poker player should always be looking to improve his play, but there is a right way and a wrong way. Specifically, if you want to make a change to your game, that change should be carefully and objectively thought out and not made on the basis of short-term results.

As we saw in chapter 3, people instinctively want to change something if they are not getting the desired results. When you are on a downswing, you will be far more likely to make an ill-advised change. This is especially true if you notice a strong short-term pattern. For example, if you notice that a particular hand or group of hands is doing especially badly for you, you might stop playing them or play them differently. Alternatively, if you have a particular play that is working well for you in the short-term, then you might start using it too frequently, or at the wrong times.

Generally speaking, you are better off not changing anything when on a downswing, until you are absolutely sure that the change is for the better. Do whatever it takes to get a second opinion, whether that is asking an expert, posting on an Internet forum, or reading the relevant

---

[36] This is covered later in the chapter.

chapter of a strategy book. When you are in an emotional slump, your instincts are less reliable than usual.

> Action Point: Immediately after your next big losing session, write down three areas where you need to improve or things that you think you need to change in your game. Put that list aside and review it after your next big winning session. Do you still believe these things need improving?

Getting obsessed with your losses

There are two main reasons why downswings are difficult to handle. The first, as already outlined, is the loss of confidence, and the second is the actual monetary loss you experience. You can lose large amounts of money very quickly, and this can affect you badly on a number of fronts.

First, there is the superficial concern about the value of money. As discussed in chapter two, some players, particularly inexperienced ones, may have a tendency to think about what could have been bought with the money they have now lost. Second, even if you aren't sensitive to the actual value of money, the money lost during a downswing can represent a considerable portion of your bankroll. While having an appropriate bankroll for the limit you are playing will help, all this will really do is minimize the likelihood of completely wiping out due to a downswing. You will still have to cope with the fact that you now have a smaller bankroll. For many players, their bankroll is their way of keeping score. Losing a large portion of their bankroll can seem like the equivalent of their poker career going backwards.

It is important that you do not get obsessed with your losses. Although it may hurt that your bankroll is now significantly smaller, you have to look beyond that. If you are obsessed with where you were rather than with where you are, you are likely to try too hard to get back there. Not only can this be demoralizing because of the scale of the task, but it is also a distraction from your primary goal. As has been repeatedly stressed in this book, the only thing that matters at the table is making the best decisions.

Try to concentrate on where you are now. Don't think about where you were or what you've lost. Think of every session as a fresh start. There is no use crying over what is no longer yours.

Trying to ride out the downswing somehow

As already discussed, there is no point trying to predict the course of a downswing, because they are random by nature. Despite this, many players come up with creative solutions to ride out a downswing. This may involve not playing for a set period of time to see if the downswing has gone away when they get back to the table, or dropping down a limit to restrict their losses until the downswing finishes.

There is no way to ride out a downswing. If you stop playing for a week and come back, you have just as much chance of getting better luck as you would if you carry on playing tomorrow. If you drop down a limit, maybe your luck will change right away and you will win less as a result. That is not to say either of these things is bad to do during a downswing. Taking a break can allow you to return to the tables more focused and less depressed. Dropping down a limit can help restore your confidence in easier games. However, to do either under the pretense of riding out the downswing is more than a little futile.

Moving up a limit to recoup your losses

This is quite possibly the worst mistake you can make while on a downswing. The idea of moving up a limit might seem crazy to you at this moment. You are in the middle of reading a book about controlling your emotions, and you are confident that it will be an easier task in the future. However, months from now when you are desperate to get back on track, the higher limits might seem like a very tempting way of trying to get your bankroll back to where it was.

This can be a fatal mistake, one that can end poker careers. Playing at a higher limit than your bankroll can withstand, even if it's "just until I get my bankroll back to its former level," is exceedingly dangerous and can wipe out your bankroll completely. Not only are you playing over your bankroll, but you are also doing it at the worst possible time: Your confidence is low, your game could well be off due to tilt, and the competition will be harder than you are used to.

Note that this mistake is especially easy for an online player to make. For a live player, moving to a higher limit involves physically moving to a different table in front of the regulars who will wonder why you are moving up. An Internet player, on the other hand, can play at a higher limit with a simple click of a button. He can make an impulsive decision and can be playing a new limit in under a minute.

5.4. Dealing with a Downswing

So if all of the above are bad responses to a downswing, then what is an appropriate response? That is the question that the rest of this chapter will answer. Of course, there is nothing that you can do about bad cards, cold decks, and suck-outs that tend to define a bad downswing. What you do have control over is your own attitude and the way you play.

You cope with downswings the same way you deal with anything else in poker. You make the decisions that will make you the most money in the long term.

Not only does this apply at the table, but also to the decisions you make away from the table. What games you play, what limits you play, and how you prepare will all play a crucial part in ensuring you come through this tough period.

One of the biggest problems with downswings is that they feed on themselves. Depression can set in during a downswing, and generally you do not play good poker when you are depressed. If you are not playing well, then your results will deteriorate, magnifying the effect of the downswing, which in turn makes you even more depressed. This cycle can continue until either:

a) You have a lucky run of cards pulling you out of the downswing; or

b) You go broke.

The best way to combat this vicious circle is not to let it start in the first place. It sounds basic, but you must make sure your play doesn't deteriorate while you are on a downswing. Of course, this is easier said than done, and will involve careful planning and strict discipline.

When you are running well

It is a good idea to prepare for a downswing before it happens. You won't be able to prevent it, but you can at least ensure that you are in the best possible frame of mind when it happens. Having the correct attitude toward your bankroll and your win rate when you are running well will help you maintain that attitude when things inevitably go bad.

First, don't fall into the trap of thinking that the good times will last forever. When running well, many players assume they can maintain that win rate indefinitely. Learn what a good win rate is for the game you play, and convince yourself that anything over that is just through the luck of the cards.

Second, it is important to have good bankroll habits while you are running well. Learn what the appropriate bankroll is for your game and don't cheat on it. When you are running well, recommended bankroll limits appear very conservative. It seems you couldn't possibly require so much money as an insurance policy. Naturally, when you are running badly, the wisdom of a conservative bankroll becomes all too apparent. If you start to cheat on your bankroll when you are running well, those habits will carry over when you are running badly. You will be tempted to play at a higher limit than your bankroll dictates in order to get your money back.

Initial reaction

So you are properly prepared and a downswing hits; then what? First of all, downswings don't "hit" exactly. As discussed earlier, downswings don't really exist as an entity in themselves. You can never say that a downswing has started. You might experience a couple of losing sessions, but that doesn't necessarily mean you have started a downswing. You might bounce back and win the money back straight away.

There's no defined point of losing when you can say, "Now I'm officially on a downswing." In fact, being on a downswing is more a state of mind than an objective reality. You lose money over a series of sessions, so you decide you are on a downswing. If you were perfectly in tune with the Poker Mindset, then you might instead say, "I have recently been experiencing some poorer-than-average results due to variance." In fact, by labeling it as such, you would have demonstrated an understanding that would indicate you are likely to respond well anyway.

But we're human and can't always see as clearly as that. Poker players have embraced the word "downswing" to indicate a period when recent results have been poor, so we'll go with that. For lack of a better phrase, what do you do when you suddenly find yourself on a "downswing"?

The first step is not to panic. You can get through it, but you will need a clear head and the ability to objectively tackle the problem. When you panic, you lose the ability to think clearly, and this behavior can lead to emotional rather than logical decisions. Remember that you are not alone. Going through a downswing seems like the worst thing in the world to an inexperienced player, but it is something that every poker player goes through from time to time, even the top professionals. Browse through poker forums on the Internet and you will find countless stories of players who are running badly. In fact, the "running bad" story is almost as prominent as the bad beat story in poker circles.

By putting yourself in the right frame of mind, you will be better equipped to deal with a downswing. It may be helpful to consider the whole ordeal as a challenge or an experiment. Make up your mind that you are not going to be the player complaining about his bad run. You are going to be the player who takes the rough with the smooth and comes through unscathed.

5.5. Staying in Control

There is nothing you can do to influence the cards you receive or the hands you and your opponents make. Your luck will improve when it improves, and that is all there is to it. This leaves you two things to concentrate your energies on during a downswing: improving your game and avoiding tilt.

If you manage to avoid tilt throughout your downswing, then congratulate yourself. You have managed to do the single thing that is most likely to limit the damage caused by the downswing and allow you to emerge from it faster. Of course, it is rarely that simple. Tilt and downswings are two topics that go hand in hand. Tilt causes downswings, which cause tilt, which causes downswings.

The relationship between tilt and downswings is a vicious circle, and either can be the trigger.

Most of us will be unable to avoid tilt completely during a downswing, so the best we can hope for is to limit its effect. In the next chapter, we will talk extensively about tilt, but in this section, we just look at the way tilt affects you during a downswing.

The reality of tilt

When players think of tilt, they often think of a player getting angry or upset and spewing chips everywhere in a fit of rage. The reality is that tilt is usually far more subtle than this. You can go on tilt without ever knowing it, even with the benefit of hindsight. Being on tilt simply means playing worse than usual in some way.

This makes preventing and detecting tilt very difficult, especially during a downswing. You will be so concerned about the money you are losing that you may not notice that your play has subtly deteriorated. Yet when you are on a downswing, you will be more susceptible to tilt than at any other time. Subconsciously or otherwise, you will be more concerned about recovering your losses, or not losing too much, and less concerned about making correct decisions.

Types of tilt you can expect on a downswing

Of course, not everybody reacts the same way to any given situation, and as such, it is impossible to say with any certainty how a particular individual will respond to a downswing. One player might start throwing caution to the wind, gambling it up to try to get his money back. Another might start playing very conservatively, subconsciously resigning himself to losing and trying to lose as little as possible. A third player might be comparatively unaffected, but will play too long, resulting in him playing while tired or bored, in hopes of recouping his losses.

While individual responses may vary, certain patterns do exist for players on a downswing. A more detailed synopsis of the various types of tilt and how to stop them is contained in the next chapter, but here is a summary of the most common traps that can befall a player running badly.

Trying to get even – Sometimes the thought of yet another losing session can prompt you to keep playing to try to get even. This generally leads to playing too loosely, or sometimes playing on autopilot when bored or tired.

Damage limitation – If you are on a downswing, you may be subconsciously trying to lose less rather than win. This might mean you play too passively or maybe too tight.

Unwillingness to gamble – None of your high-risk, high-reward plays ever seem to work, so you stop making them. You play too tightly or too passively, refusing to play speculative hands or make bluffs.

Breaking the pain threshold – Sometimes you will be running so badly that you simply don't care any more. You have lost so much that you figure losing more won't hurt. The result is that you play too loosely or too aggressively, or both, which are very destructive forms of tilt.

Any of the above has the potential to reduce or even reverse your positive expectation. Fortunately, we have the tools to stay in control during downswings. They are the same tools that we use to cope with most psychological adversity in poker. We are of course talking about the Poker Mindset.

5.6. Downswings and the Poker Mindset

Preventing tilt when on a downswing is all about attitude. If you play poker in the correct frame of mind, you are less likely to tilt. The Poker Mindset will help you see the downswing for what it is. Let's look at it piece by piece.

Understand and accept the realities of poker – Poker
is a high-variance game. What you are experiencing is nothing scary; it is just the inevitable bad period to correspond with the good periods you experience.

Play for the long term – Your downswing is just a short-term
downturn in results and not significant to your long-term plan.

Emphasize correct decisions over making money
– If you are making the correct decisions, then the fact that you are losing is irrelevant. If you aren't making the correct decisions, then you had better concentrate on that rather than on any bad luck you are experiencing.

Desensitize yourself to money – The money you are
losing is unimportant. If you are making the correct decisions, then you should be happy.

Leave your ego at the door – Don't take this downswing
as an affront to your ego. Don't try too hard to get even, or delude yourself into thinking you can play at a higher limit than your bankroll allows.

Remove all emotion from decisions – If you are making
decisions logically and without emotion, then you won't be tilting.

Dedicate yourself to a continuous cycle of analysis and improvement – Face it, your game needs
work. Stop feeling sorry for yourself because of the bad luck you are experiencing and do the one thing you can do to improve your results: Learn to play better!

The Poker Mindset is the key to avoiding tilt during a downswing. Read it before playing during a downswing. If you have to, photocopy it and take it to the casino (or tape it to your monitor if you are an Internet player). Read it whenever a downswing is getting you down or when you feel yourself tilting due to bad results.

In fact, the last part of the Poker Mindset deserves further scrutiny with respect to downswings. Studying hard to improve your game is the one proactive thing that you can do during a downswing. It is such an important concept that we will dedicate a section to its discussion.

5.7. Improving Your Game

One of the most difficult things to do while on a downswing is to assess objectively how well you are playing. Of course, if you are playing perfectly, then a downswing is absolutely nothing to worry about. All you need to do is to keep playing and wait for your luck to turn around.

But no one ever really plays poker perfectly. No matter how well you think you play, you can always improve your game. Therefore, when you are on a downswing, your bad play is partly to blame, even if you are not tilting at all and are still playing as well as you were before the downswing hit. Generally speaking, you should remember the following two things when you are on a downswing.

1. It is very unlikely that your downswing is entirely due to bad play.
2. Likewise, it is very unlikely that bad play is not contributing to your downswing at all.

Studying to improve your play is very important when on a downswing. If you reduce the "poor play element," and improve your win rate, you will recover more quickly.

Let's illustrate this with some figures. Say you are playing limit Hold'em and have a long-term win rate of 1.2 big bets per 100 hands. You play on the Internet, and your sessions are always 200 hands long (for simplicity's sake). In each session you would expect to earn 2.4 big bets on average. Of course, you won't earn exactly 2.4 big bets per session (or this whole chapter would be redundant).

In a 200-hand session, you could potentially make more than 40 big bets, or lose the same amount.

However, what if you increase your win rate to 1.5 big bets per 100 hands? Now you would expect to earn 0.6 big bets more every session. The following table shows a rudimentary series of ten sessions. In the middle column, player A has a win rate of 1.2, and in the right column, player B has a win rate of 1.5. The chart represents the same ten sessions (same cards, opponents, etc). The amounts won are in big bets and are mostly negative to simulate a downswing.

Session	Amount Won (Player A)	Amount Won (Player B)
1	-20.3	-19.4
2	-10.9	-11.1
3	+5.0	+5.1
4	-26.3	-27.5
5	-2.6	-1.3
6	-13.6	-12.3
7	+30.4	+29.2
8	-26.1	-24.2
9	-1.7	-1.5
10	-13.9	-11.0

Look at the two columns of results. They both look similar, and at a glance, it is difficult to see which player has lost more. You will notice that there are some sessions where player A has actually won more (or lost less), despite the fact that his win rate is lower. This is entirely possible in poker; bad play is regularly rewarded in the short term. Neither player would be particularly happy after this period, and the differences in results are almost invisible, consumed by the magnitude of the overall swing.

However, if you add up all the results, you will note that player A lost 80 big bets, while player B lost only 74 big bets.[37] That difference of six big bets can be significant over the long term, and on average that is how much the better player B will do *every ten sessions*. The longer the downswing goes on, the bigger the difference will be. If player A goes on a downswing lasting 30 sessions, he can expect to lose 18 big bets more than player B. If after 25 sessions more he is fully recovered, player B would already be fully recovered and have made an additional 33 big bets (which at $15-$30 limit, for example, would be about $1,000).

Hopefully, this has illustrated the importance of improving your play. It is necessary at all times, but especially while you are on a downswing. Improve your win rate when you are running well, and you will win more money. Improve it during a downswing and not only will you win more (or lose less), but you will also bottom out at a higher level and recover more quickly, reducing the likelihood of tilting.

Improving your game when on a downswing

The difficult thing about improving your game during a downswing is that identifying leaks is more complicated. When you are on a downswing, *nothing* seems to be going right, so it might be tough to identify where you are making errors as opposed to where the cards just aren't falling your way. Pay special attention to how you collect your data. Make sure you are not inadvertently making a decision based purely on results since you have been running badly. Naturally, when you are running badly, certain hands and plays that would otherwise be profitable appear to be unprofitable.

---

[37] This is what we would expect on average. The better player will expect to win 0.6 big bets more per session, and there are ten sessions, so he would expect to earn 6 big bets more on average over this period.

There are two types of errors you might be making while on a downswing:

Inherent errors – These are flaws in your game that have always been present. Correcting these flaws will increase your overall win rate and help you come out of the downswing faster. It will also allow you to sustain a higher win rate in the long term after the downswing is long forgotten. These are good errors to fix.

Derived errors – These are specific mistakes that you are making as a result of being on a downswing, or, to put it another way, these errors are by-products of being on tilt. Such mistakes make it difficult to come out of the downswing, because they can dramatically cut your win rate. In fact, while playing on tilt, you might no longer be a winning player at all. Fixing these errors is vital, but it is far better to "cut them off at the source," as it were, by stopping yourself from tilting in the first place.

While finding and correcting leaks in your game is an end unto itself, it also has fringe benefits. First, by concentrating on improving your game, you are keeping your mind on something other than your poor results. Much of the problem with downswings comes from dwelling on your results between sessions to the point where you don't expect to win when you sit down. If you don't expect to win, then it is often a self-fulfilling prophecy, not for superstitious reasons but because you are subconsciously playing defensively to minimize your losses.

In addition, by proactively improving your game, you can sit at the table with greater confidence, knowing your game is better than when you last played. Although the difference might be small, anything that strengthens your belief that you can win is a good thing.

5.8. Downswings and Your Bankroll

Like tilt, the topic of bankroll management is integral to any sensible discussion of downswings. When you are on a downswing, you must carefully consider its impact on your bankroll and make the appropriate decisions. Your bankroll is the one thing that keeps you in the game, and the chance of a downswing becoming fatal is directly proportional to the strength of your bankroll and your ability to make sound decisions to protect it. In fact, bankroll management is a vital skill for any winning player, which is why we dedicate an entire chapter of the book to the topic.

Your bankroll is always relative to the limit you are playing. For example, a $3,000 bankroll is probably plenty if you are a $3-$6 limit (or $100 no-limit) player, but woefully inadequate if you regularly play $15-$30 (or $500 no-limit). Obviously, if you are looking to move up a limit, you should not do so until you have the bankroll for that new limit. For example, if you play a 300 big bet bankroll strategy in limit Hold'em, and you are a $5-$10 player, then you should not move up to $10-$20 until you have $6,000 (300 big bets at the new level).

Even more important is remembering to move down limits at the right time. Your bankroll will naturally shrink during a downswing. If the downswing is large enough, there is a risk that you are not sufficiently bankrolled to play at your current limit and should move down.[38] Unfortunately, players on a downswing are often bad at moving down limits, which can be for a number of reasons:

1. It's a step backwards.

The psychological impact of moving down limits can be quite severe. This is a particular problem for players who have successfully managed to desensitize themselves to money by keeping score in limits rather than money won. The higher the limit they play, the better they feel they are doing. Dropping down a limit is their equivalent of taking a big step backwards.

---

[38] This is also discussed in detail in chapter 7.

2. It will be harder to win back losses.

Players who understand downswings (or are just optimistic) tend to stay mindful of the fact that the next session could be the one that gets them back on track. It can be painful for these players to drop down a limit, because they realize that if the next session is a big win, they will only win a fraction of what they would have had they played at their current limit.

3. The player might be in denial.

Some players are reluctant to drop down a limit because they refuse to accept that their bankroll is in fact smaller. Most winning players are mindful of their "max bankroll", which is the highest their bankroll has ever been. When they have less than that, they still remember that figure even though it is now irrelevant.

For example, let's say a limit Hold'em player has a bankroll of $3,000. He plays a 250 big bet bankroll strategy and so is happy playing $5-$10. Then he goes on a minor downswing, losing 100 big bets. He now has a bankroll of $2,000 and should drop down to $3-$6, but he doesn't see it that way. He believes that he's having a period of bad luck (true) and that in time he will receive good luck to compensate (not true). Therefore, there is no need to drop down a limit (not true). As far as this player is concerned, he has every right to play $5-$10 still because *he is a $5-$10 player*!

While this seems like a strange way of thinking, it is the way that many players do think, some without even realizing it. If your bankroll is $2,000, then it is $2,000 regardless of what it may have been in the past. There is no sense in treating it any other way. That "former high point" figure of $3,000 is completely irrelevant to any calculation of your bankroll requirements.

Cheating on your bankroll

Of course, when you cheat on your bankroll, the only person you are cheating is yourself. Bankroll recommendations are what they are for a reason, and if you play at too high a limit for your bankroll, then you run the risk of going bust. This is especially true during a downswing, as you may well be playing worse than normal, making it more likely that you will continue to lose.

If you are thinking of cheating on your bankroll requirements during a downswing, don't, no matter what your reasoning is. The human mind will come up with all kinds of clever justifications for doing something you want to do. If you cheat on your bankroll, *you are risking your entire poker career*. In a few months' time, your downswing will be in the past and forgotten. Unless, of course, you elected to fudge your bankroll requirements, in which case you may well be out of the game. The choice is yours.

Action Point: Visit a poker forum such as InternetTexasHoldem.com and spend a while reading the posts from players who are on downswings. As a third party, try to objectify their experiences in your head. While reading their posts, see if you can discern any mistakes in attitude or mindset that the poster seems to be making.

5.9. Chapter Review

❑ **5.1. Running Badly**
- A downswing is a period when a player earns significantly less than their expected win rate over a number of sessions.
- The high variance in poker makes it inevitable that you will suffer sustained losses from time to time. These will not be rare, freak occurrences, but something that most players have to put up with regularly.

❑ **5.2. The Reality of Downswings**
- Downswings are not an entity in themselves, but an observed pattern in results.
- A common error is trying to assign downswings properties, such as giving them a fixed size, shape, or frequency.
- Many players try to define downswings in the present or future tense. They are trying to predict future events based on past results, which is impossible.
- Unfortunately, the psychological pressure of running badly for a sustained period of time makes ignoring downswings difficult.
- Managing a large downswing is one of the most difficult things you will have to do as a poker player, and the penalty for failure can be losing your entire bankroll.

❑ **5.3. Common Bad Responses to Downswings**
- These are some of the most common bad responses to downswings:
  - Losing confidence in your ability and game
  - Making radical changes to your play
  - Getting obsessed with your losses
  - Trying to ride out the downswing
  - Moving up a limit to recoup your losses

❑ 5.4. Dealing with a Downswing

- You cope with downswings the same way you deal with anything else in poker. You make the decisions that will make you the most money in the long term.
- Your decisions away from the table such as what games you play, what limits you play, and how you prepare will all play a crucial part in ensuring you come through tough periods.
- If you are not playing well, then your results will deteriorate, magnifying the effect of the downswing, which in turn makes you even more depressed. This cycle can continue until either:
  - a) You have a lucky run of cards pulling you out of the downswing; or
  - b) You go broke.
- Having the correct attitude toward your bankroll and your win rate when you are running well will help you maintain that attitude when things inevitably go bad.

❑ 5.5. Staying in Control

- There are two things to concentrate your energies on during a downswing: improving your game and avoiding tilt.
- The relationship between tilt and downswings is a vicious circle, and either can be the trigger.
- Some of the most common traps that can befall a player running badly include:
  - Trying to get even
  - Damage limitation
  - Unwillingness to gamble
  - Breaking the pain threshold

❑ 5.6. Downswings and the Poker Mindset

- Preventing tilt when on a downswing is all about attitude. If you play poker in the correct frame of mind, you are less likely to tilt.
- Understanding the seven attitudes of the Poker Mindset is the key to avoiding tilt during a downswing.

❑ 5.7. Improving Your Game

- Generally speaking, you should remember the following two things when you are on a downswing.
  1. It is very unlikely that your downswing is entirely due to bad play.
  2. Likewise, it is very unlikely that bad play is not contributing to your downswing at all.
- If you reduce the "poor play element" of a downswing, and improve your win rate, you will recover more quickly.
- While finding and correcting leaks in your game is an end unto itself, it also has fringe benefits helpful in recovering from a downswing:
  - By concentrating on improving your game, you are keeping your mind on something other than your poor results.
  - By proactively improving your game, you can sit at the table with greater confidence.

❑ 5.8. Downswings and Your Bankroll

- If a downswing is large enough, there is a risk that you are not sufficiently bankrolled to play at your current limit and should move down.
- Unfortunately, players on a downswing are often bad at moving down limits, which can be for a number of reasons:
  1. It's a step backwards.
  2. It will be harder to win back losses.
  3. The player might be in denial.
- If you cheat on your bankroll, *you are risking your entire poker career.*

Chapter 6

Tilt

"Poker is a combination of luck and skill. People think mastering the skill part is hard, but they're wrong. The trick to poker is mastering the luck." – Jessie May (from *Shut Up and Deal*)

Tilt is a topic that has cropped up in every chapter of this book so far, as it is integral to the subject matter. Nearly every aspect of the Poker Mindset is in some way related to reducing the impact that tilt has on your game. This chapter looks at why players go on tilt, and categorizes different kinds of tilt while looking at their most likely causes and effects. We will look at ways to avoid tilt, and what to do if you notice that tilt has crept into your game.

6.1. What Is Tilt?

Tilt is simply the act of playing worse than you are capable of playing. To go on tilt means that your play has deteriorated in some way. At its core, this is a simple definition, but tilt has many layers and nuances, which can sometimes make it difficult to detect.

Tilt is not the same as bad play. Thousands of players play extremely badly, not because they are tilting but because they don't know any better. Tilt implies that the player in question has both the ability and the desire to play better, but for some reason is not currently playing his best.

Some people have a very narrow idea about what tilt is, the most common being:

- Tilt involves steaming off a large amount of chips through excessive betting and raising.
- Tilt involves playing too many hands and calling too many bets with weak or mediocre holdings.

Although both of these are quite plausible, there are many other ways that a player might go on tilt. Thinking of tilt as only steaming or chasing is a very limited view. Tilt is any deviation from your best game; it does not always involve a major change in your play. In fact, we will see in the next section that there are six distinct types of tilt. A player might go on tilt without him or his opponents even knowing it.

Nearly every player suffers from tilt at some point. Some players are more disciplined than others, and you will sometimes meet players who claim they never tilt. The truth of the matter is that maybe they don't tilt very often or very badly, or don't even notice when they are on tilt. Every player has, at one time or another, made a call that he knew he shouldn't make, seen a flop with a hand he knew he should muck, or made a play without taking proper account of the exact game state. It is nearly impossible to play your absolute best for every hand in every session.

The important thing to remember is that not all tilt is created equal, and its effect can vary greatly. Tilt often has only a minor impact on results, but sometimes it can lead to the deterioration of a player's game into a loose uncontrolled mess. The impact it will have on your game will depend on a number of factors:

Type

Some forms of tilt are naturally more destructive than others. For example, if you are playing too tightly pre-flop, the worst that can possibly happen is that you lose the blinds/antes every round. On the other hand, loose tilt can involve you playing way too many hands, which can have a significant impact on your bankroll. Later in the chapter we'll look at different types of tilt and their relative danger.

Severity

Even the same type of tilt can be more or less destructive depending on how large the change in your play is. If your play is only subtly different, then it will obviously be less dangerous than if you are playing extremely badly.

Duration

The amount of money you lose through tilt is directly proportional to how long you tilt for. If you only play one or two hands badly, then the effect is unlikely to be catastrophic, especially in limit poker. If you tilt for a long period or an entire session, the results can be severe.

Game type

Generally speaking, tilt is more harmful to no-limit or pot-limit players than to limit players. The freedom to make and call large bets effectively gives you the freedom to make bigger mistakes.

These factors make it impossible to say definitively how dangerous tilt can be. The result could be anything from a barely noticeable decrease in your expected winnings to the complete elimination of your bankroll, or anything in between.

The reason tilt is so important is that your edge in poker is small, and anything that erodes that edge further will have a serious effect on your bottom line. Even if you have the technical skills to be a strong winning player, it doesn't take much for you to turn into only a marginal winner, a break-even player, or even a losing player.

Many players have the technical skills to be long-term winners, but their lack of the correct Poker Mindset prevents them from achieving long-term success. In essence, they tilt away all of their winnings.

Professional poker players play their best game frequently — if they did not, they wouldn't survive. But players with the ability to make a lot of money playing poker can ultimately go broke because they cannot control their tilt. This phenomenon is similar to what you observe in many other sports. Sometimes very promising players cannot make it at the top level, not because they lack the skill or physique, but because they lack the intangibles necessary for success. They might lack the discipline to achieve greatness or they might let their egos prevent them from performing their best. The player who cannot control his emotions in the heat of battle will certainly choke when the pressure is on.

6.2. Why Do Players Go on Tilt?

This is not an easy question to answer. Every player is different and will have different reasons why he goes on tilt. A situation that puts one player on tilt may not affect another player at all. But we can make generalizations about why certain types of tilt are common and what situations might trigger it. To do so, we must peel back a number of layers and look at what influences the way people play poker.

Think back to how you played the first time you sat at the poker table. How did you instinctively feel the game should be played? Most players starting out will play too loosely. Their line of thinking goes something like:

The best poker players are the ones who win the most money.
The way I win money is to win pots.
I can't win pots when I fold.
Conclusion: I must play a lot of hands to be a good poker player.

New players tend to play too many hands even when given the advice not to. These same players often continue too long after the flop, chasing weak draws in hopes of winning a hand. It takes a lot of discipline, learning, and experience before a new player understands correct poker strategy and realizes that what is important is not winning pots but winning money.

New players will also instinctively play too passively. When they play a hand, they tend to check and call rather than bet and raise — unless they have a monster. They will try to get to a showdown cheaply to "see if they've won" but are unwilling to take a lot of risks unless they are confident they have the best hand. Once again, it takes a lot of learning and discipline before a new player understands the value of aggression when playing a hand.

New players also tend to make plays without considering all the variables. They play their own hand without considering their opponent's possible holdings. They certainly won't consider complex variables such as position, pot odds, and the betting patterns of their opponent. It is hard work to consider every variable every time you make a decision, and you need to be disciplined to keep this up every hand.

Instinctively, players like to play loosely, passively, and without due consideration of the game state. It is no coincidence that when players go on tilt, the three most likely ways they do so is to play too loosely, too passively, and too formulaically.

In effect, tilt is often (but not always) a regression of a player's game to something more primal. He temporarily loses the discipline that controls his game and instead starts making decisions in accordance with how he would like to play the game.

What causes players to revert to this undisciplined poker? If we can understand why players go on tilt, then we will be far better equipped to recognize when we are likely to tilt. Traditionally, tilt is thought to be an emotional response to negative stimuli. For example, a player would go on tilt as a result of taking a bad beat, losing a big pot, or losing a lot of money. However, this is just a stereotype, like saying that tilt *always* involves steaming or excessive calling. Although bad beats and downswings are a major cause of tilt, they are by no means the only ones. All of the following can initiate or contribute to tilt.

- Any emotional state (not just the stereotypical anger, depression, and self-pity)
- Fatigue or tiredness
- Boredom
- An unusual game state
- An abnormal series of results
- Alcohol

In other words, tilt is not only something that you need to watch out for when things are going bad; it's something you must be constantly wary of.

Think of poker as a war within yourself, the classic heart versus head battle. On one side is your heart telling you to play the game the way you would like to play. It urges you to see the flop with second-rate hands, "peel one off" on the flop with a weak holding, or call down rather than raise with a strong one. On the other side is your head telling you to play the game the way it should be played, urging you to make the moves that will maximize your long-term profits, even if it means concentrating extra hard or making plays that you would rather not make.

For most players under normal circumstances, your head gets the casting vote in poker decisions.[39] *However, that other voice is always there, urging you to take a different line.*

For some players, that voice will be very quiet, so they will be less likely to go on tilt. For other players, the voice is loud. It might not be

---

[39] Note that we say "most players." Occasionally, you find players who know how to play well but nearly always play badly. Effectively, they are permanently on tilt.

quite loud enough to overrule the head under normal circumstances, but it will take charge if anything happens to make that voice louder, or the message from your head quieter or less certain. For example:

- You take a bad beat. Your heart encourages you to gamble more to give yourself the chance to get that money back.
- You are playing at a higher limit than usual. Your heart highlights the additional exposure to your bankroll and encourages you to play more cautiously and passively, in order to avoid a potentially big loss.
- You are bored. Your heart encourages you to watch football after each fold when you should be observing your opponents.
- A maniac is throwing his weight around. Your heart tells you to confront him head on, to constantly re-raise him pre-flop and show him who is really in charge of the table.

These are only four out of dozens of possible scenarios. You are no longer making the best decisions, because they are now controlled by your heart and not your head. You might not realize that you are playing badly. Sometimes the two voices can get very confusing, and you might not realize until after the event how badly you were playing.

In summary, tilt is simply a state where players, for whatever reason, lose their ability to think through decisions and make the best play. Tilt can be a short-term thing, even lasting only one decision, while other times the effect will last many hours or even multiple sessions. No player is safe from it because every player has that voice, however quiet, somewhere within his conscience.

6.3. Different Types of Tilt

There are six distinct types of tilt, which we categorize in terms of how your play is affected. Some of these are more common than others, while some are more harmful. In this section, we will go through each category and discuss how it might affect your play, how serious it is, and what its likely triggers are.

In the previous section, we saw how tilt often reflects how we would like to play the game. Hence, the three most common types of tilt see players returning to the bad habits they had when they first started playing, before they learned how to play well. These are:

Loose Tilt
Passive Tilt
Formulaic Tilt

In addition, there are three less-common forms of tilt:

Aggressive Tilt
Tight Tilt
FPS Tilt[40]

They are less common because they involve playing in a way that is not natural to most people, and also because the triggers for them don't happen too often. Although they are not as common as the other three forms of tilt, individual players may be especially prone to one of these rarer types. For example, a naturally nervous and risk-averse player might be prone to tight tilt more than any other kind. A hot-headed player with a large ego might be especially prone to aggressive tilt.

---

[40] Stands for "Fancy Play Syndrome," a phrase first coined by Mike Caro.

Loose Tilt

Loose tilt is probably the most common form of tilt and involves playing too many hands pre-flop and not folding frequently enough post-flop. The main reason why this type of tilt is so common is that it involves playing in a way that we would all secretly like to. Most players don't genuinely enjoy folding 75% of their hands before the flop. Poker is far more fun when you are actually involved in the action.

In fact, because nearly all players would like to play more hands than they know they should, it doesn't take much to convince a player to do so. For this reason, there are many possible triggers for loose tilt, the most common of which are as follows.

Trying to get even – If you are "stuck," the temptation is always there to try to get even for the session. Not only will you play longer than you intended, but you will also be tempted to play more hands, hoping to hit the big one that gets you back to even for the session. Before the flop, you will be tempted in the wrong situations by speculative hands that might hit big, like suited connectors and small pairs. After the flop, you will be more prone to chase long-shot draws, such as gut-shot straights, when the pot odds don't justify a call. In essence, you will start to gamble with plays that have a negative expectation in the hopes of getting your money back.

Frustration – If you have taken one too many bad beats, you might start playing too many cards and chasing weak draws. Frustrated players will often find themselves trying to win a pot to get back on track.

Impatience – There are times in poker when you will receive cold cards for a sustained period. You will get dealt such garbage that when you do eventually get a hand such as K-T off-suit or Q-7 suited, it looks like a monster. Rather than sticking to your starting hand rules, you will start playing marginal hands that you usually fold.

Overconfidence – When you are running incredibly well, you might start to overestimate your own ability. You will start to believe you are invincible rather than correctly attribute your unusually high win rate to luck. At this point, you might start playing more hands, thinking you can outplay your opponents after the flop. While this may be true to an extent, there is a point where your post-flop skills cannot compensate for the weak hands you are entering pots with, especially in limit Hold'em.

The damage done by loose tilt depends on how loosely you play and for how long. Fortunately, if your play is only slightly off, you will probably only be playing marginally unprofitable hands and calling slightly too often after the flop. These types of mistakes will only cost you a small amount on average. If you tilt badly, though, the damage is potentially limitless. Playing too loosely is the single mistake most likely to lose you money consistently over the long term.

Passive Tilt

Passive tilt is a poker player's silent enemy. It can creep into your game without your noticing its arrival, and once there, it can be difficult to detect. Rather than betting and raising in the right situations, you will begin to check and call too frequently. Passive tilt generally affects a player's post-flop play more than his pre-flop play, as pre-flop raising is normally something that is done automatically from rule.

Passive tilt is nearly always caused by either a loss of confidence or latent risk aversion. The most-likely triggers are outlined below.

Running badly – A bad session might make you less inclined to bet and raise your good hands. Subconsciously, you will begin to expect the worst and that your opponent will always hit his draw. To minimize your losses when that "inevitable" bad card falls, you will stop betting and raising. In addition, you will tend to go into check/call mode when faced with any aggression from your opponents unless you have an extremely strong hand.

New limit – When you play a new higher limit for the first time, you might be less willing to raise, because the monetary amounts involved look much higher. You will become conscious of the amount of money you could potentially lose if things go wrong. You will also be likely to give the players at this new limit more respect, even if their play doesn't warrant it. Subconsciously, you will consider them better than you, until you get used to the new limit and believe you belong.

Insufficient bankroll – Players with an insufficient bankroll will have a tendency to play too passively because they are unable to properly absorb downswings. They can't afford to take high-variance gambles with positive expectation, or at least they will feel that way.

A big problem with passive tilt is that it can go undetected for a considerable period of time, especially when simply triggered by running badly. Ian once had a 250-big bet downswing and decided to send his hand histories to a friend for analysis. His friend pointed out several hands where he had missed bets and raises, and it became apparent to Ian that he had been on passive tilt.

Passive tilt can be a big problem because it feeds on itself. If you take a few bad beats and go on passive tilt, you might not protect future hands properly. This gives your opponents the chance to draw out on you even more, which might force you even more into your shell. Before you know it, you are a tight, passive rock, with no positive expectation.

Formulaic Tilt

Formulaic tilt simply means that you are playing "by the book" without adapting to the game. In essence, you are effectively playing on autopilot, without thinking hard enough about the specific situation you are in. For example, you might fold A-J to a raise, a standard play, but you don't notice that there are no other callers and the raiser has raised nine out of the last ten pots. Another example is folding a mediocre hand on the button even though both blinds are extremely tight and almost never defend. In other words, you will be playing uninspired and predictable poker.

Some players might not consider this a type of tilt, but it most certainly is. Going back to our definition, tilt is the act of playing worse than you are capable of playing. When you let things distract you and don't adjust to the game, you are on formulaic tilt. The most common triggers of formulaic tilt are as follows:

Boredom – When bored, we all know that our mind starts to wander and we are easily distracted by other things. When boredom sets in during a poker game, you will start to do the minimum you think is necessary to beat the game, rather than trying to beat it for the maximum possible. Poker is a game of small edges. A player who is generally a winning player could turn into a losing one when he loses focus, or at least win a lot less.

Tiredness – Tired people cannot concentrate as well as rested people. The more tired you are, the harder you will find it to concentrate, which results in playing your cards more than playing your opponents' tendencies.

Distractions – In a similar vein as the triggers of tiredness and boredom, any distraction will prevent you from focusing 100% on your play. In a casino, the distraction could be anything from your team playing on the TV to an obnoxious player sitting next to you. Internet players have a whole minefield of potential distractions, including the Internet, email, phone, TV, or a family member or friend talking during play.

Something on your mind – Distractions can also come from within. You lose focus when you are thinking about other things going on in your life not related to the poker game at hand. This is especially true when you are not actively involved in the hand, as your mind will start to wander.

Contempt – Sometimes formulaic tilt is caused by not having sufficient respect for the game you are playing. This might be because you have just moved down a limit to a game you consider beneath you or because you have consistently beaten the same game for a long period of time. Whatever the reason, you won't concentrate fully when you think you can win by simply going through the motions.

Fortunately, formulaic tilt is usually not too costly, at the lower limits at least. If you are a winning player, you should still be able to beat the game, albeit at a lower expected earn rate. In fact, many Internet players play many tables simultaneously in a formulaic way to increase their overall earn rate, even though their earn rate per table is less.[41] Once again, no-limit players have to be more careful because each mistake can be more costly. For example, an "easy fold" to a large bet by a rock might turn into a call if you weren't fully aware that the player was a rock.

The danger of formulaic tilt is that it can affect your every decision and is something that can creep into your game as a natural inclination. If you play against weak players, you can win by playing on formulaic tilt, which means it can be habit-forming. The more you play on formulaic tilt, the harder it will be to concentrate in the future. While you may still be winning, you will not be fulfilling your potential, nor will you be developing some of the finer skills of the game. When it comes to moving up limits, you may get a rude awakening as to how lackluster your game really is.

Aggressive Tilt

A player on aggressive tilt will overplay his hands, betting and raising where he should just be checking and calling, or even folding. The triggers for true aggressive tilt are uncommon for most players but unfortunately all too frequent for others.

---

[41] Obviously, at this point it can no longer be considered tilt, as it is now a conscious decision.

Losing it – Sometimes you can get so emotional, so angry, so upset, or so depressed that your results no longer have any real meaning. You have moved beyond pain into a world where the money you lose no longer hurts. You spew chips into every pot you enter, raising with reckless abandon.

Vendetta – In the course of the game, another player might do something that annoys you enough so that you want to get even. If this happens, you will be in danger of playing too aggressively against that player, subconsciously trying to assert your authority over him.

Overreaction – Sometimes you will just get it into your head that you need to be more aggressive. In many cases, it is just a knee-jerk reaction to some recent negative results. Whatever the reason, it can be quite easy to overdo it when it comes to aggression. You start raising too often and in the wrong circumstances. Later you may well look back on the session and wonder exactly why you raised in certain situations.

The good news about aggressive tilt is that it generally doesn't last for very long and is comparatively easy to detect. The bad news is that, pound for pound, it is probably more dangerous than any other type of tilt in the short term. It can cost you many bets on each round of betting, and if you suffer from a bad dose, it can erode your stack extremely quickly, especially in big bet poker.

Aggressive tilt is especially devastating when combined with loose tilt. Suffer from both at the same time and you are really in trouble. This is most likely to happen when you "lose it" as described above.

Tight Tilt

To be on tight tilt means to fold too often. Pre-flop you will not play hands that have a positive expectation, while post-flop you will turn down profitable draws and fold too many made hands. Tight tilt is probably the rarest form of tilt because very few players actually enjoy playing tightly, so there is very little temptation to do so. The problem for most players is playing *tightly enough*.

Despite this, there are a number of possible triggers for tight tilt, which are as follows:

Similar to passive tilt – Tight tilt is similar in nature to passive tilt in that it tends to be caused by a lack of confidence. Although passive tilt is far more common, all the triggers of passive tilt could potentially also cause tight tilt. If you have recently experienced bad results, are playing at a new, higher limit, or are playing above your bankroll, then be on the alert for tight tilt.

Protecting a win – In the same way that some players tend to chase losses when they're stuck, some try to protect wins too much when they're ahead. They will tighten up and only play premium holdings, and even then they try not to get sucked into pots where they are not a strong favorite. This can be especially true when a player doing well is just waiting for the blinds to get to them before they leave.

Bad results with a hand – Sometimes when a player has a string of bad results with a particular hand or group of hands, he will lose faith in that hand, even if it has historically had positive expectation for him. For example, a player who has missed a long string of flush draws in a row might start folding them after a while, especially if he is a conservative, risk-averse player by nature.

Tight tilt is the least dangerous form of tilt. Nothing disastrous tends to happen because of money you don't put in the pot. In fact, if you know that you're on tilt but can't quit the game for some reason (for example, you are in a tournament), then playing too tightly can be a good makeshift solution until you manage to pull yourself together.

The only manifestation of tight tilt that can really cost you a lot of money is folding too much on the river. You only have to make this mistake a few times in a session to seriously reduce your win rate.

FPS Tilt

"Fancy Play Syndrome" is a phrase used by poker players to describe plays that are too complicated and deceptive. While the idea behind them is usually sound, it would be better to simply make the straightforward, obvious play. Often this is just a one-off occurrence, but sometimes a player will start to make too many fancy plays over a period of time. At this point, he can be said to be on FPS tilt. In some ways, FPS tilt could be considered the opposite of formulaic tilt. The player tends to over-think situations rather than not think enough.

The most common manifestations of FPS tilt are bluffing too much and slow-playing too often. While both bluffing and slow-playing have their uses, they are weapons that go blunt if they are overused. Some players also have particular tricks that they are proud of — the delayed bluff on the turn, the bluff-raise on the river, the limp followed by a re-raise. Unfortunately, they will start to use these tricks whenever they can, eventually getting to the stage where their surprise factor (the whole point of them in the first place) is lost. The following are the most common triggers of FPS tilt.

Overconfidence – Sometimes when you are running well you will start to believe your own hype. Everything you try is working, so you start trying crazier and crazier things, not realizing that you are winning in spite of your unconventional play, not because of it.

Trying to make things happen – When you are running badly, it is often tempting to try and "make things happen" by running bluffs. Your thought process goes, "I'm not getting any good hands, so I have to try and win somehow." Of course, this reasoning is flawed. If the play has positive expectation, you should have been doing it anyway; if not, then it is a bad idea to start now.

Bad table – Sometimes when you are at a bad table (one filled with good players), you will attempt to rise to the challenge rather than leave and find a better table. You will bluff too much, slow-play too much, and generally outthink yourself.

FPS tilt is not terribly common, but like the other rarer forms of tilt, some players are particularly prone to it. You will probably know if you are the kind of player who likes to make fancy plays or not. This tendency is not terribly harmful as long as there are solid strategic reasons for why you are attempting those plays. However, FPS tilt is very difficult to detect, and as a result, it can slowly chip away at your win rate without it ever being recognized. Unfortunately, it often occurs along with loose tilt, which can be an expensive combination.

> Action Point: Try to identify the types of tilt that you are prone to and what your individual triggers are.

6.4. Preparing for and Avoiding Tilt

One important lesson to learn from the previous section is that tilt is not a one-dimensional phenomenon. Some players imagine tilt as a line with "good play" at one end and "bad play" at the other, where your point on the line indicates whether you are tilting and by how much. This is not a helpful way of looking at it.

Tilt is a lot more two-dimensional. A better, more accurate way to think about tilt is to imagine it as a circle with a mark representing good play in the middle of the circle and all the different kinds of tilt around the outside. Your job is to stay in the middle and not move toward the edge, even though there are forces pulling you in all directions.

You don't want to give into temptation and play too loosely, but then again you don't want to go too far the other way and play too tightly. It is important not to let yourself become passive, but being too aggressive could be even more dangerous. You must focus on the game and use every tool at your disposal, but not to the extent of making too many fancy plays. Avoiding tilt is a constant balancing act, which is why so many players fail at this task.

The fight against tilt is a three-step process. The first is to take precautions to minimize the possibility of tilt. The second step is to learn how to recognize when you are on tilt, and the third is to act appropriately if you find that you are. The first step is the most important. It is much better to deal with tilt before it arrives than to try and deal with its consequences once it has already done its damage.

There are a number of steps you can take to minimize your chances of going on tilt. If you adopt the Poker Mindset outlined in chapter two, you will have an excellent head start on this process. You will see that many of following concepts are directly or indirectly linked to what we learned in chapter two.

Ensure you are properly bankrolled

An adequate bankroll is fundamental to poker success, not just for preventing tilt. If your bankroll is strong, you can more easily rationalize any losses you experience. You will never feel in danger of going broke and will feel less pressured to get even. This liberates you from the stress and pressure that may put you on tilt.

Choose your playing times carefully

Don't play poker when you are upset.
Don't play when you have something big on your mind.
Don't play when you are tired.
Don't play when you can't focus 100% on the game.

This is simple advice that you should always follow. Ideally, when you play poker, you want to be in a confident (but not overconfident) mood. You want to be fully awake and alert while looking forward to playing, with nothing on your mind that may distract you. If you're not, then you will not be in the best frame of mind to play your best game. You will be more likely to be distracted, which can lead to tilt.

You should be wary of using poker as a release from problems elsewhere in your life. While many of us play poker to unwind and relax, you shouldn't play if there is something serious on your mind. If you do, you will go on tilt far more easily because you are already emotionally unbalanced. You might lose a heap of money and add one more thing to your list of woes.

Don't keep score

Most players are guilty of keeping track of how much "up" or "down" they are for the session, but you should try to avoid keeping score in this way. There is no advantage to it; the best decision is the best decision, regardless of how well you have been doing in the session.[42] Keeping score just encourages you to go on tilt, because you know when things are going badly or, for some people, when things are going well.

Treat every decision as independent

Each decision should only be made with the intention of making the highest expected earn rate in the long term. If anything else plays a part in making a decision, you are tilting. Every decision must be treated as independent. Whatever happened on previous hands is in the past, whether you took a bad beat, won a huge pot, had an argument with another player or anything else. As Doyle Brunson eloquently put it:

"Try to decide how good your hand is at a given moment. Nothing else matters. Nothing!"

This doesn't mean that you shouldn't remember how players have acted in the past; of course you should. It's just that this information

---

[42] In big bet poker, you do need to keep track of your stack size. However, there is a difference between keeping track of your stack for the purposes of making better decisions and keeping track of your stack so that you know how much you have won or lost.

should only be used to make your decision a better one, not as an excuse for making a play that you know you shouldn't.

Have the correct attitude toward your opponents

From one point of view, your opponents are your enemy. It is your goal to win their money and their goal to win yours. Much poker literature uses the metaphor of battle and war when talking about a game of poker, and indeed this is a valid comparison.

However, if you take a different perspective, your opponents aren't really the enemy at all. While it is true that their collective success is inversely proportional to your own, they are really just another part of the game, which you must adapt to. Your goal isn't to beat your opponents; it is to win the most money, which can only be done by making the best decisions possible.

The only one who can prevent you from making the best decisions in a poker game is yourself.

If you look at poker as a war, then subconsciously you will be trying to prove to your opponents that you are better than them in order to win the war. Your ego starts to make your decisions rather than your brain, and this can put you on tilt. You are desperate to recover your losses, prove a point to your opponents, or target a particular opponent you perceive as your nemesis. If you believe in the metaphor that poker is a war, try to leave it as a metaphor and don't bring a war-like bloodlust to the table.

Note how many of these ideas are related to the Poker Mindset. By adopting the attitudes in the Poker Mindset, you will be taking a big step toward protecting yourself from tilt before you even sit down at the table. If you accept the realities of poker, you will know in advance the likelihood of bad beats and bad sessions and are less likely to react badly to them. By emphasizing correct decisions over making money, you are less likely to keep score and more likely to treat each decision as independent. By leaving your ego at the door, you will foster a better attitude toward your opponents.

6.5. Detecting Tilt

The first step in the battle against tilt is to do everything possible to prevent yourself from going on tilt. However, if you lose this battle and tilt *does* creep into your game, then you need to move onto the next step. Step two is to recognize when you are on tilt, which can be trickier than you might think, for two reasons. First, the change in your game might only be slight, almost unnoticeable. Second, if you are emotionally charged enough to tilt, there is a chance your emotions are also clouding your ability to objectively assess your play.

It is imperative to constantly be on the lookout for signs of tilt when you are playing. This chapter has given you a good idea of the most common types of tilt and their causes. As you gain more and more experience, you will also start to learn what your individual triggers are. As we stated earlier in the chapter, different players react badly to different things. Unfortunately, you do not know what might trigger tilt in your own game until it happens. Be aware of the following signs that you may be on tilt.

Emotions – What kind of emotional state are you in right now? Are you particularly sad, angry, worried, depressed, or have another emotion dominating your mood? The emotion might be related to the game or to something else, but the result will be the same. Even if you think it isn't affecting your play, it probably is.

Bad plays – Sometimes you will have enough poker wits about you to realize that you are making bad plays. You might look back at the previous hand and recognize that you made a bad play with no good explanation. Congratulations, you have just realized that you are on tilt — move onto step three. You have to be a little bit careful how you define bad plays. Sometimes a decision looks bad in hindsight, but at the time, your decision was made for the right reasons. Try to think back to what your thought processes were at the time of the decision and see if they were reasonable.

Wayward thinking – If you notice yourself making a play for any reason other than maximizing your expectation, then stop to consider the possibility that you are on tilt. Did something starting with one of the following phrases go through your head when you made the decision?

> I should fold this, but....
> I am stuck/ahead this session, so...
> He/she is getting on my nerves, so...
> I have been running badly/well lately, so...

If so, then you are almost certainly on tilt.

Lack of focus – Are you thinking constantly about something other than the game? Is the dealer (or the "bleep" on the Internet) occasionally having to remind you that it's your turn? Are you not really enjoying playing right now? If so, it is likely that you are not playing your best game.

Inconsistency – Did you just make a decision that was different from one made before in similar circumstances? If so, stop to consider if there is a good reason for the change. If not, then you are on tilt.

Reactions of others – When you are badly on tilt, sometimes you will notice the attitudes of your opponents change. They might start targeting you with their play or whispering to each other while looking in your direction. Players who normally respect your play might start making fun of you. Alternatively, a friend who is observing the game might mention to you that you are playing badly. If any of these things happen, you probably are unable to assess your own play, so just assume you are on tilt and move straight to step three.

Spotting any of the above could tell you that you are on tilt, or at least give you a reasonable suspicion. If you are unsure, it is always prudent to assume that you are tilting until proven otherwise. Better to be safe than sorry.

Action Point: Try to spot when your opponents are on tilt. Look for any of the above signs in their play or demeanor. By doing this, not only will you be able to exploit their weaknesses, but you also will become more aware of the same problems in your own game.

6.6. Combating Tilt

What do you do once you are aware that you are on tilt?

If you are on tilt, stop playing!

This is the golden rule of tilt. Combating tilt is step three of our process and is by far the easiest to master. It is so easy, and yet so many players manage to get it wrong. They will say something like:

I knew I was tilting, but...

...It wasn't affecting me too badly.
...The game was so good.
...I was still playing well enough to beat the game.
...I had nothing else to do for the next couple of hours.
...I wanted to try to get my money back.
...I promised myself I would play x hands tonight.

This can be disastrous thinking. Playing poker while not playing your best game is, at best, a marginal proposition, or at worst, a huge money drainer. A winning player's edge is small enough already, without reducing it further by playing on tilt.

It sounds so simple, but when it comes to tilt, players seem to think they can win money regardless of the fact they are playing at a disadvantage. It is possible to win at poker when playing on tilt if the effect is only minor. In that case, you may still have some kind of edge left.[43] It's a big risk, though, for the following reasons:

- Players tend to overestimate their edge. While you might think you can still outplay your opponents even while on tilt, this is not necessarily the case, especially when you consider the rake.
- It is difficult to pinpoint how badly you are tilting. You may have noticed that you are on tilt, but are you aware exactly how much? Maybe you are tilting in other ways that you don't realize.
- Tilt often escalates as the session goes on. While you might be able to beat the game now, if your game deteriorates further, you could start to bleed cash.

In reality, playing while on tilt is a dangerous game. If you notice that you are tilting, quit the game now and be glad that you caught yourself in time. Head home and don't stop at the craps table, the slots, or anywhere else where you might be tempted to steam off money.

Action Point: On the Internet, you can play poker at extremely low limits. Some players use these "micro-limit" games as an outlet when they are on tilt. They can play on one of these tables and play extremely badly with no real financial repercussions. Losing $5 at a $.05-$.10 limit game is a lot better than losing $1,500 at a $15-$30 game. If you are an Internet player, try this the next time you suspect you are on tilt.

---

[43] Hence, once you are a very experienced player, it *might* be advantageous to continue playing while on minor tilt. You won't be able to play your A-game all the time, but sometimes your B-game will be good enough. However, for the purpose of this discussion, always quitting at the first sign of tilt is excellent advice that you would be well advised to follow. It can be extremely difficult to gauge exactly how much of an edge you have left.

6.7. Tilt in Tournaments

With every rule there seems to be an exception. Tournaments are unique in that you might go on tilt after you have already made a financial commitment to the tournament. In this case, you need to somehow make the best of the situation and try to maximize your expectation.[44]

By far the most common cause of tilt in tournaments is when a player with a big stack takes a bad beat and loses a large portion of it. The feeling of being one of the chip leaders and then suddenly only having an average or even a short stack can be too much for many players to take. How you lost the pot might have some bearing on how it affects you. Some players get mad when they take a bad beat, while others get angrier when they make a mistake that costs them chips. Players in this situation often go on tilt, start leaking chips, and bust out of the tournament shortly thereafter.

There are a number of ways to help protect yourself against tilting in these circumstances. While on tilt you will be prone to making bad decisions, so your aim is to minimize the number of difficult decisions that you are forced to make, until such time as you are able to play your best game again. Here are some tips for achieving that objective:

Take a break

If you are really steaming, your best bet might be to leave the table and take a walk. Spend 10 to 20 minutes just taking a stroll, getting some fresh air, or watching another table, whatever you fancy. When you return to the game, try to think of it as a fresh start. You might also try thinking about a particular tournament in which you did well when you were able to fight back with a small stack. Generally, the situation is not nearly as bleak as it might seem at first. You're still in the tournament, which is better than being busted out, so make the most of it.

---

[44] Here, we are talking about regular tournaments with no rebuy, or rebuy tournaments after the rebuy period has expired. If you bust out of a rebuy tournament during the rebuy period while on tilt, then the "just quit" rule still applies.

Tighten up

Maybe you are not tilting badly enough to need to leave the table, but you're not in a position to play your best game. In this case, tighten up and wait for tier-one premium hands before you enter a pot. Your opponents might be caught off guard by this change in gear, especially because players on tilt usually start playing *more* hands. You might get paid off if you hit a big hand and your opponents assume you are steaming.

Action Point: If you play in a lot of tournaments, then try this: Next time you lose a substantial portion of your stack in a tournament, declare the next orbit a cool-down period. Do not enter the pot unless you hold AA, KK, QQ, or A-K. This will prevent you from doing anything stupid and give you some time to get your concentration and focus back.

Obviously, during this time you will have long periods with nothing to do but watch and think. Use this time to calm down and refocus your mind. Watch other players and see what you can learn. Who is the table bully? Who are the weak players? Who is on a rush? Who is losing and how is he coping? Think about all the things you should be thinking about rather than your own predicament. Eventually, you should feel ready to rejoin the game playing your best poker.

Play ABC poker

If you are slightly on tilt, it is not the time to try fancy plays, big bluffs, and clever traps. By simply betting your hand, you give yourself less opportunity to make bad decisions. Very few players will pick up on the fact that you are now playing ABC poker, especially if you usually have a reasonable level of deception in your game.

Play pre-flop

If you are going to struggle to make the right decisions, the best way to play is one in which you have to make as few tough decisions as possible. Put yourself in a position where it is your opponents who have to make the tough decisions, not you. Raise or fold pre-flop rather than call, and, if you are playing big bet poker, raise slightly more than usual to give yourself a better chance of winning a small pot rather than losing a big one.[45]

Of course, the plus side to tilting in a tournament is that you can never lose more than your tournament buy-in; whereas in a cash game, you could potentially lose a lot of money, maybe even your entire bankroll, through tilt. On the downside, if you tilt late in a tournament you could potentially cost yourself a chance at a big payday which is much higher than even your current bankroll. If you do bust out of a tournament through tilt, then head home, study *The Poker Mindset*, and vow not to make the same mistake again.

6.8. Chapter Review

❑ **6.1. What Is Tilt?**
- Tilt is simply the act of playing worse than you are capable of playing.
- Tilt is any deviation from your best game; it does not always involve a major change in your play.
- The impact that tilt has on your game will depend on a number of factors:
  - Type
  - Severity
  - Duration
  - Game type

---

[45] Note this is the same strategy that is recommended when you are playing against players better than you. In his book *Tournament Poker for Advanced Players*, David Sklansky outlines an extreme version of this system in which with every hand you either go all-in or fold before the flop.

- Many players have the technical skills to be long-term winners, but their lack of the correct Poker Mindset prevents them from achieving long-term success. In essence, they tilt away all of their winnings.

❑ 6.2. Why Do Players Go on Tilt?

- Instinctively, players like to play loosely, passively, and without due consideration of the game state. It is no coincidence that when players go on tilt, the three most likely ways they do so is to play too loosely, too passively, and too formulaically.
- In effect, tilt is often (but not always) a regression of a player's game to something more primal.
- Think of poker as a war within yourself. On one side is your heart telling you to play the game the way you would like to play. On the other side is your head telling you to play the game the way it should be played.

❑ 6.3. Different Types of Tilt

- Loose Tilt - Loose tilt is probably the most common form of tilt. It involves playing too many hands pre-flop and not folding frequently enough post-flop.
- Passive Tilt – Passive tilt is when you begin to check and call too frequently.
- Formulaic Tilt - Formulaic tilt simply means that you are playing "by the book" without adapting to the game.
- Aggressive Tilt – Aggressive tilt is when you overplay your hands, betting and raising where you should just be checking and calling, or even folding.
- Tight Tilt – To be on tight tilt means to fold too often.
- FPS Tilt - "Fancy Play Syndrome" tilt occurs when you over-think situations and start to make plays that are too complicated and deceptive.

❑ 6.4. Preparing for and Avoiding Tilt

- The fight against tilt is a three-step process:
  1. Take precautions to minimize the possibility of tilt.
  2. Learn how to recognize when you are on tilt
  3. Act appropriately if you find that you are on tilt.
- There are a number of steps you can take to minimize your chances of going on tilt.
  - Ensure you are properly bankrolled
  - Choose your playing times carefully
  - Don't keep score
  - Treat every decision as independent
  - Have the correct attitude toward your opponents

❑ 6.5. Detecting Tilt

- Recognizing when you are on tilt can be trickier than you might think:
  - The change in your game might only be slight, almost unnoticeable.
  - If you are emotionally charged enough to tilt, there is a chance your emotions are also clouding your ability to objectively assess your play.
- Be aware of the following signs that you may be on tilt:
  - Emotions
  - Bad plays
  - Wayward thinking
  - Lack of focus
  - Inconsistency
  - Reactions of others

❏ **6.6 Combating Tilt**

- The golden rule of tilt: If you are on tilt, stop playing!
- Playing poker while not playing your best game is, at best, a marginal proposition, or at worst, a huge money drainer.
- It is possible to win at poker when playing on tilt if the effect is only minor. It's a big risk, though, for the following reasons:
  - Players tend to overestimate their edge.
  - It is difficult to pinpoint how badly you are tilting.
  - Tilt often escalates as the session goes on.

❏ **6.7. Tilt in Tournaments**

- Tournaments are unique in that you might go on tilt after you have already made a financial commitment to the tournament.
- While on tilt you will be prone to making bad decisions, so your aim is to minimize the number of difficult decisions that you are forced to make. Here are some tips for achieving that objective:
  - Take a break
  - Tighten up
  - Play ABC poker
  - Play pre-flop by raising or folding rather than calling

Chapter 7

Looking after Your Bankroll

"Money management is, in some ways, much more important than talent." – Annie Duke

7.1. The Biggest Mistake in Poker

So far in this book we have covered a lot of ground, but one subject we keep returning to is your bankroll. Quite simply, good bankroll management is one of the most important skills you will learn when playing poker. In fact, poor bankroll management could be considered the biggest mistake in poker.

What is bankroll management?

Bankroll management is simply the practice of ensuring that you have enough money to play poker for the long term. Throughout the book we have reminded you that poker is a game of high variance. Although playing good poker will win you money in the long term, anything can happen in the short term, and the short term is a lot longer than you might think. In chapter five, we discussed how this variance can lead to downswings when you will lose money over a sustained period of time.

If you play winning poker, these downswings will be offset in the long term by periods when you run abnormally well. The only problem is that if you run out of money during a downswing, you will never get a chance to *reach* the long term because you will be broke and out of the game. The essence of bankroll management is making sure this does not happen.

Unfortunately, it is impossible to be absolutely safe. A downswing can be any length, and no matter how large your bankroll, there is always a small chance that you could lose it all. However, if you follow a sensible bankroll strategy, you can reduce this to a freak outside chance rather than a very real threat.

Of course, bankroll management is really only something that applies to winning players. A losing player can never have enough money to cover his downswings because he has negative expectation. In the same way that a winning player plays for the long term, the long term is the enemy of the losing player. A losing player will always lose his bankroll eventually no matter how large it is. All a losing player can do as far as bankroll management is concerned, is play at as low a limit as possible so that his money lasts longer.

If a losing player wants to win money, his only hope is to win in the short term and then quit the game forever.[46] This is, in essence, what most people hope for when they take a gambling trip to Vegas. Everyone knows that the house wins in the long run, but there is always the possibility that you can get on a lucky streak over a weekend and go home with more money than you arrived with.

Psychology and your bankroll

We have been talking about a simple truth: Lose your bankroll and you are out of the game.[47] This is the main reason that bankroll management is so important. But there is more to it than that.

It is not only the actual risk of losing your bankroll, but also the fear of losing your bankroll that we need to contend with.

Every player has this simple truth seeded somewhere in their subconscious. From the perspective of the Poker Mindset, you will be far better equipped psychologically to play your best game when you have a sufficiently large bankroll behind you for the size of game

---

[46] Or improve his game to the point where he can win, of course.
[47] At least until you can find some money to replenish it.

you regularly play in. Consider some of the key elements we have emphasized in this book:

Correct decisions over results
Desensitize yourself to money
Indifference to losing individual pots
Calmness and objectivity through downswings

These attitudes are easier to adopt when you have a sufficiently large bankroll. Let's illustrate this with some numbers. Would you say that $1,000 sounds like a lot to lose in one session at the poker table? Of course, your answer to this will depend on the limits you are used to. A low limit player would consider it a large loss, but if you were playing a $10-$20 limit or $2-$4 no-limit cash game, then this kind of loss would be perfectly normal. If you play even higher limits, then you would experience even higher losses on a regular basis.

But what difference could the size of your bankroll make? If your bankroll were only $2,000, then this result would be a disaster. You would have just lost half your bankroll in one session, and that is something any player would be extremely concerned about. But what if your bankroll was $30,000? That $1,000 is now almost a drop in the ocean. You will be disappointed to lose that money, but you can put that result in perspective knowing that it only represents a tiny portion of your bankroll.

This can make all the difference between starting your next session in a confident, relaxed mood and starting it in fearful knowledge that another similar session will wipe you out completely.

If the fear of going broke is preying on your mind, then this is likely to lead to bad decisions at the table.

You might naturally play defensively and be unwilling to exploit small edges. Or worse, you might begin to play looser, subconsciously trying to win back the money you lost in the previous session. It is difficult to play your best game knowing that you are dangerously close to busting out. As discussed in the previous chapter, tilt is an enemy that is never far away, and a strong bankroll is an important defense in your battle against it.

In fact, you could argue that good bankroll management is more fundamental than the Poker Mindset in ensuring your success at the table. Without good bankroll management, the Poker Mindset becomes much more difficult to substantiate.

Play for the long term – But without a strong bankroll, there may not be a long term to play for.

Emphasize correct decisions over making money
– But when you go broke due to a sharp downswing, it is little consolation that you busted out while making correct decisions.

Desensitize yourself to money – But how can you when one bad session could wipe you out completely?

In short, the attitudes in the Poker Mindset are the building blocks for success at the table, but they can only be achieved on a foundation of sound bankroll management. The remainder of this chapter explores the issue of bankroll management from a number of angles. We will define what a good set of bankroll rules might be and look at why players are often bad at bankroll management. We will then look at the issues of moving up limits, moving down limits, and cashing out.

7.2. Determining Your Bankroll Requirements

A great deal has been written by others about how big your bankroll should be, so this is not an area we are going to spend a lot of time on. But, to make sure we are all on approximately the same page, it is useful to outline a basic bankroll strategy. We are not saying that this system is definitively the one you need to follow, but it is a sensible, conservative bankroll strategy that will not put you too far wrong.

Base level bankroll

When working out your bankroll strategy, a sensible place to start is with a default base level. The figures below for the three forms of poker are a starting point. You need to take the relevant figure and modify it according to the variables listed later in this section.

Limit poker – Your base level for limit poker is 300 big bets, a big bet being the size of the bet after the turn (in Hold'em or Omaha) or after 5th street (in Stud).

Big bet poker – For big bet poker (both pot limit and no-limit), your base level should be 20 buy-ins. By buy-in, we mean the maximum permissible buy-in at the table where you are playing. A buy-in is usually around 100 times the big blind. If it is lower, you will need to increase this number.

Tournaments – Your base level for tournaments should be about 75 buy-ins; a buy-in being the total cost of entering the tournament. Because multi-table tournaments have a higher variance than single-table tournaments that have become popular online, sit-n-go tournament players could probably reduce this number to 40.

Modifications

The above figures are reasonable guidelines for the size of bankroll you will need for various poker games. However, they need to be modified according to your specific circumstances and games. Generally speaking, the higher your win rate and/or the lower your variance, the smaller the bankroll you will need. Here is an idea of some of the variables that might affect your bankroll requirements.

Game – Some games require a larger bankroll because they tend to have a higher variance. For example, Hold'em players tend to experience much larger swings than Omaha hi-lo players.

Opponents – If you play against tight and passive opponents, you will usually experience smaller swings than if you play against loose and aggressive opponents. You will therefore need a larger bankroll against the latter.

Number of Players – Shorthanded games tend to have a much higher variance than the equivalent nine- or ten-handed games. Heads-up games have a greater variance still. The fewer players in the games you play, the larger the bankroll you will need.

Win rate – A marginal winner will experience larger downswings than a player with a higher win rate[48] and so will need a larger bankroll. As stated previously, a losing player can never have a large enough bankroll. If you are relatively new to the game and don't have an established win rate, you should increase your bankroll because your win rate is probably not as high as an experienced player's (even though you might currently be experiencing excellent short-term results).

Acceptable risk – Bankroll management is about reducing risk. You can use a smaller bankroll if you are willing to accept a larger possibility of going broke.

---

[48] This was illustrated in chapter 5.

Cashing out – The bankroll requirements above assume that you will grow your bankroll rather than cash out your winnings. If you cash out all or part of your winnings, you will need to increase your bankroll requirements accordingly. This is discussed in detail later in the chapter.

Dropping limits – If you are willing to drop limits quickly when on a downswing, you can get away with a smaller bankroll than if you have a built-in buffer zone within which you will not drop down. Again, this is discussed in more detail later in the chapter.

Action Point: Using the above figures and the suggested modifications, calculate what you think would be a sensible bankroll for you to play with at your current limit. If this is significantly larger than your current bankroll, consider moving down a limit to better protect yourself against downswings. There is a bankroll calculator tool at InternetTexasHoldem.com to help you determine a baseline bankroll based on your limit, win rate, and variance.

Two extreme examples

To illustrate the impact that the above factors can have on your bankroll, let's consider two players, Adam and Steve. Both are limit players and both are long-term winners, but other than that, they are very different.

Adam is a low-limit player and plays Omaha hi-lo. He plays in full ring games at his local casino, where the opposition is very weak. He is a good player but plays mainly for recreation; he already makes good money at his day job. In fact, if Adam lost his entire bankroll, it wouldn't be the end of the world for him, because he doesn't see the cash amounts as significant. His bankroll could easily be reimbursed with his own money.

Steve is a professional poker player and plays high-limit games on the Internet. He is very strong player, but his win rate is only modest because he is mostly playing against other strong players. He plays a range of games and is often forced to play short-handed due to a lack of a good full ring game. He withdraws a fixed wage each month to live on, and if he has a bad month, he might be forced to withdraw more than he has actually made in that month. If he lost his bankroll, it would be a disaster. He would now have no means to make money.

What size bankroll should each of these players be using? Adam will need less than the default 300 big bets. He has a big edge and is playing in a low-variance game. He also plays live, so he sometimes picks up physical tells and mannerisms that Steve could not. Adam is willing to accept a higher risk, because the money in his bankroll is not so important to him, and he is not relying on it to make a living. Adam could happily play on a bankroll of 200 or even 150 big bets.

Steve will obviously need a larger bankroll, but how much larger? His low win rate, combined with the fact that he cashes out a lot of money each month, means there will be times when his bankroll is under a great deal of pressure. He also plays short-handed, which will increase his overall variance. Steve is living dangerously if his bankroll is less than 1,000 big bets, and he may want to consider having even more for added security. The difference is really that great.

How rigid are these numbers?

As you can see from the example above, it is important to know and understand the factors that can influence the bankroll you need. Surprisingly, though, the actual numbers that you use are far less important than the discipline with which you stick to your bankroll. It is far easier to make good decisions in the face of adversity when you have a strict set of rules and protocols to adhere to. A player who has strict bankroll rules will move down when necessary and is less likely to do something foolish such as trying to recoup losses by moving up a limit.

7.3. Why Do Players Go Wrong?

You may have the impression so far that bankroll management is easy, and you would be absolutely right. There is nothing at all complicated about bankroll management. Just use a bit of common sense to determine sensible bankroll rules and then stick to them.

Why, then, do so many players manage their bankrolls badly? Why do players who have managed to conquer the difficult parts of poker fall down at what is possibly the easiest stage? Unfortunately, it all comes down to the human failings of shortsightedness, vanity, and greed. Even a player who has learned to play poker well may manage his bankroll badly for many reasons.

Bankroll recommendations seem very conservative

Bankroll recommendations can seem very conservative. A winning player who lacks experience might struggle to see how he could possibly need so much money for a bankroll. While he will certainly have had losing sessions before, he assumes that he will carry on winning at his current level indefinitely. He has yet to experience a significant downswing to fully realize the brutal realities of poker.

Players overestimate their own ability

Most poker players think they are better players than they actually are. Big-time losers think they are only slight losers who might break even if not for the rake. Small losers think they break about even, or at least they would if they didn't get so unlucky. Small winners think they win more than they do. They tend to blame the cards for not being able to earn the win rate commensurate with their limit. Even big winners frequently overestimate their long-term edge.

It is a common human weakness to overestimate one's ability, not just at poker but at everything. For example, how many people will admit that they don't deserve a promotion or a raise? When it comes to bankroll requirements, this translates into a disdain for the large sums that are often recommended. The line of thought goes something like "Other players might need that much money, but not a strong player like me."

The allure of the higher limits

No matter what limit you play at, the next one up always seems very attractive, especially when you are running well and full of confidence. Some players want to play at a higher limit in order to make more money and are willing to cheat on their bankroll requirements to do so. The human mind is excellent at coming up with a justification for something that you want to do, even when deep down you know you shouldn't.

Bad habits from the lower limits

Players at the lower limits are sometimes very blasé about bankroll requirements. In the back of their mind, they know they can reload if they need to. Unfortunately, when you get into the habit of playing with a small bankroll, it can be difficult to break that habit, especially if you are fortunate enough not to experience a large downswing while you are working your way through the lower limits. Eventually, when you do arrive at the higher limits, you could be seriously under-bankrolled and run the risk of going broke, which *would* be painful.

Acting foolishly when under pressure

Some players are good at following bankroll rules most of the time, but make bad decisions when under pressure. Maybe they are on a downswing and choose not to drop down a limit when they should. Maybe they go on tilt and suddenly choose to play in a higher-limit game, desperately trying to get their money back. There are a number of ways that a player under pressure or on tilt might commit bankroll "suicide."

No matter what the reason, it is clear that a large number of winning players are bad at bankroll management. In fact, behind the scenes, some of the famous players you see on TV are broke or relying on backers to pay their entry fees. Being a good poker player on its own does not guarantee success.

Bankroll management is not hard. It's just a case of having the right attitude coupled with learning and applying some basic rules. By adopting the Poker Mindset, you can improve your bankroll management skills by avoiding the pitfalls described above. Below are three cherry-picked sections of the Poker Mindset that relate to bankroll management.

1. Understand and Accept the Realities of Poker

Understand that poker is a game of high variance. Even the best players will have sessions and strings of sessions when they lose money. Therefore, it is imperative that they properly bankroll themselves to absorb any downswings that they may experience.

2. Play for the Long Term

Good poker players are only assured of winning money in the long term. If you play with an insufficient bankroll, you run the risk of never being able to reach the long term because you are wiped out by some short-term bad fortune.

3. Leave Your Ego at the Door

Ego often rears its ugly head when players make bankroll decisions. Players don't believe they need a large bankroll because they overestimate their skill and their edge. They will also be reluctant to drop down limits when they should because they consider playing at a lower limit to be beneath them. It is important that you leave your ego at the door and make the decisions that will maximize your winnings in the long term rather than those that will just make you feel better in the short term.

Be sure to utilize the Poker Mindset not only at the tables but also in those decisions you make regarding bankroll management even before you sit down and start playing. In the rest of this chapter, we examine other bankroll management issues as well.

7.4. Moving Up Limits

The limit you play at is always a dynamic thing. While you might have the correct bankroll for a specific limit right now, you could be one bad session away from having to drop down, or indeed one good session away from being able to play at a higher limit. In fact, most players look forward to the point when their bankroll is sufficient to play the next limit up, because the next limit up is seen to represent new opportunities, new challenges, and a new milestone in their poker career.

Of course, there is no rule that you have to move up when you have the bankroll for the next limit. Bankroll requirements only apply in one direction; there is no rule that you can't play with significantly more than the required bankroll for a given limit. Some reasons for not moving up a limit as soon as you can include:

You haven't mastered your current limit – If you haven't been at your current limit for long, then you might feel more comfortable if you play more hands at your current limit first, before moving up again. This might happen if you run unusually well for a period or if you have artificially padded your bankroll with money from a high hand jackpot, a bonus of some kind,[49] or if you just put more of your own money in.

You don't think you can beat the new limit – Maybe you have watched some games at the higher limit and are not confident that you can beat them. In this situation, it is highly responsible not to move up a limit until you believe you are at a level where you *can* beat these games. Just try not to confuse a genuine concern about the

---

[49] Cash bonuses are often given on Internet poker sites as a way of attracting or keeping players. The bonus might be for signing up, depositing more money, or playing a certain number of hands.

games being harder with the natural nervousness and paranoia you get when you move to a new limit for the first time.

You are scared by the higher nominal swings –

When you are looking to move up a limit, sometimes the higher cash amounts can seem scary. Moving up a limit is inevitably going to feel strange at first because the blinds, bets, and pots are much larger than you are used to. If your feelings go beyond simple unease to the extent that they are adversely affecting your play, you should consider going back to the lower limit until you can learn to objectify the cash amounts involved more thoroughly. Some players might encounter a threshold beyond which they will never be comfortable with the cash amounts involved. If you are one of these players, then the best thing to do is just to play as high as you are comfortable with and not worry about moving up limits anymore.

Action Point: When moving up limits, it is sometimes better to do it gradually. Start by playing a one-hour session of the new limit each night, followed by your normal limit for the rest of the night. After a week, play your new limit for two hours. This will gradually let you become accustomed to losing bigger pots without putting you at risk of a major losing session. Try this next time you move up a limit.

Whatever the reason, very little can be gained from playing in a game where you don't really want to be playing. While there is very little room for making suboptimal decisions when playing poker, choosing what limit you play at within your bankroll is a decision that is very much up to each player.

The Peter Principle of Poker

Although there is no hard and fast relationship between the limit and the difficulty of the game, generally speaking, the higher the limit you play, the tougher the games become. There are two main reasons for this. First, poor players lose money faster at the higher limits and so won't stick around as long. Second, better players tend to gravitate to the higher limits from the lower limits. Whenever you move up a limit, you should assume that the players will be better, on average, than those at your old limit. As a consequence of this, your win rate in terms of big bets is likely to take a significant hit compared to what you enjoyed before.

In the world of large corporations, there is a theory called the Peter Principle. This states that every employee will, over time, receive promotions until they reach a level where they are incompetent. The "conclusion" of this principle is that whole organizations are staffed entirely by incompetent people who are unable to do their job because they were promoted one level beyond where they could shine.

Whether or not there is any truth in this theory,[50] the Peter Principle can certainly be seen in the poker room. Players tend to start at the lower limits, and if they have the skill, they will make money and advance to the higher limits. Eventually they will reach a limit where they are no longer winning.

The Peter Principle of Poker: Poker rooms contain a lot of former winning players who have advanced to a limit that they cannot beat.[51]

Our intention in saying this isn't to discourage you from moving up through the limits. It is merely to illustrate that when moving up limits, you should always be mindful of the fact that each limit will (with occasional exceptions) be tougher than the last. Sometimes you

---

[50] Based on some of the corporations that we know, there seems to be at least some truth in it.

[51] Applying the Peter Principle to poker was originally conceptualized by Mark Blade in his book *Professional Poker*.

will move up a limit and then find that you can't beat the game at that limit. At this point, one of three things will happen:

1. You move back down to your old limit.
2. You stubbornly decide to stay at your new limit and eventually go broke.
3. You improve your game to a level where you can beat the game at the new limit.

Obviously, the last of these is what you should be aiming for. Once more, this takes us back to the Poker Mindset:

Dedicate Yourself to a Continuous Cycle of Analysis and Improvement.

It's possible that you might move up to a game at a limit that you just can't beat no matter how much effort you put into improving your game. If you reach this point, then you are obviously better off dropping down to a limit where you can win, rather than stubbornly sticking with the higher-limit game. Go back to the games that you can beat, and make money there rather than falling victim to the Peter Principle of Poker.

7.5. Moving Down Limits

Moving down limits is far less exciting than moving up, but infinitely more important. If you are running badly to a point where you no longer have a sufficient bankroll for your current limit (by your own rules), then you should drop down a limit. If you carry on playing at your current limit regardless, then you are in no better shape than if you never had a bankroll rule in the first place. In fact, you may well be in worse shape, because your downswing may have put you on tilt. Being in denial can delude you into thinking that you can play at a limit higher than your bankroll dictates.

Most players hate dropping down limits for the same reason that they like moving up limits. It represents a step backwards in their poker career. Consciously or otherwise, it is considered a defeat or an admission of failure, and their ego does not like it. Your ego might make you feel embarrassed when others see you playing the lower limit and *know* that you are running badly. It may give you some comfort to know that even the best players have to drop a limit once in a while, and they hate it, too. How often do you hear poker players say something like:

> I was playing $15-$30 while waiting for the $30-$60 game to start.
> I couldn't find a good $10-$20 game, so I played $5-$10 instead.
> I usually play $20-$40, but today the $15-$30 game was exceptionally juicy.

There is nothing wrong with any of these reasons for playing a lower limit, but why do they feel the need to tell you *any* reason? It's because players feel attached to their usual limit. Subconsciously or otherwise, they think the lower limits are beneath them. If they're telling you about something that happened in a game that was below their usual limit, then you can be darn sure that they will want to tell you *why* they were playing at a lower limit. In fact, it's quite possible that the real reason why they have dropped a limit is that they are running badly and are no longer bankrolled for their usual game, but they are embarrassed to say it.

It is natural not to want to drop down a limit, and it is common to be embarrassed when you have to do so. Obviously, if you fully embrace the Poker Mindset, it wouldn't bother you at all because you would recognize that variance makes dropping limits inevitable. However, it is not vital that you have this "perfect" attitude, merely that you swallow your pride and drop down.

Buffer zones

To help prevent cheating on your bankroll requirements, incorporating some downward inertia into your bankroll plans makes sense. For example, instead of having a hard bankroll rule of 300 big bets for limit play, you could move up to a new limit when you hit 320 big bets, but only drop down when you no longer have 280.

There are several benefits to this strategy. First, it allows a player running badly to play a bit longer at his current limit without having to actually cheat on his bankroll. Remember, the actual numbers you use for your bankroll are less important than the fact that you are disciplined about sticking to them.

Second, this strategy prevents too much flip-flopping. Sometimes when your bankroll is on the cusp of a new limit, you may find yourself going backwards and forwards between the two limits. This is not only frustrating but can actually be detrimental to your game because you are unable to focus on one limit and get used to the game and the players there. Sometimes there are even minor rule changes to get used to. For example, flip-flop between $2-$4 and $3-$6, and you constantly have to adjust between a small blind that is one half the amount of the big blind and a small blind that is one third the amount of the big blind.[52]

We encourage players to build buffer zones into their bankroll plan if they so wish, but with two caveats:

1. The level at which they drop down must still be realistic. A buffer zone larger than 20% is definitely not recommended.
2. A player shouldn't invent a buffer zone when he is in the middle of a downswing. Make a rule from the start and stick to it.

Provided these two rules are adhered to, buffer zones can be a good thing.

---

[52] In a $3-$6 game, the small blind is generally only $1.

7.6. Cashing-out Strategies

If you are a successful player, a time will come when you start to think about cashing out so that you can enjoy some of your winnings. If, when, and how you should do so is not clear-cut because of conflicting interests. On one hand, you would like to keep growing your bankroll so that you can play at higher and higher limits and see potentially bigger wins in cash terms. On the other hand, there is no point in doing this if you never get to reap the rewards of your labors. After all, unless you are a regular in the big game at the Bellagio, there is always a higher limit to shoot for.

There is no hard and fast rule about cashing out. Experienced players tend to recommend waiting as long as possible before you start cashing out, but this is usually based on their own experiences. If you are making $50 per hour in a $30-$60 game, then you would probably regret the time that you stunted your growth by cashing out your winnings when playing $5-$10. Conversely, maybe you don't have the skill to make $50 per hour playing $30-$60. Then you would be far better off making some supplementary income playing $5-$10 than trying to reach a limit that you can't beat.

When, and how much, you cash out is really up to you. There is no correct cashing-out strategy, although there is such a thing as an incorrect one. Look out for the following errors when you consider cashing out:

- Cashing out more than you make each month on average. Naturally, this will cause your bankroll (and hence, your potential earn rate) to shrink over time.
- Cashing out meaningless amounts. Online players can play at limits where the cash amounts are so small that they are not worth cashing out. What qualifies as "meaningful" will naturally vary from player to player, but let's just say that if

you make $10 playing $.05-$.10, you are probably better off using this money to build your bankroll and move up limits, rather than cashing it out.

- Never cashing out. If you are making a lot of money at poker and never cash out, then you are probably missing the point of poker somewhere. Growing your bankroll may be one of your goals, but the game is far more enjoyable when you get to spend your winnings on something real. Reward yourself for your hard work from time to time.

- Falling victim to the Peter Principle of Poker. It doesn't make much sense not to cash out in order to move up to a limit where you are perpetually treading water in a game you can't beat. If you get to a point where, despite your best efforts to improve, you still can't win, then it may be better to play at a lower limit and start cashing out your winnings.

- Not incorporating cashing out into your bankroll strategy. Remember, the more you cash out on a regular basis, the larger your bankroll will need to be to insure yourself against a large downswing.

Often the best way to compromise between growing your bankroll and cashing out is to adopt a mixed strategy, whereby you cash out some of your winnings and use the rest to grow your bankroll. You can tinker with the proportion that you cash out to suit your own needs and priorities. A player who wants to cash out most of his winnings while still allowing his bankroll to grow slowly might cash out 80-90%. A player who just wants to drip-feed himself a little of his winnings might cash out only 25%.

The important thing is that you find a system that works for you. Bankroll management, moving up and down limits, and cashing out are dependent on the individual to some degree. We can provide general guidelines, but every player has different needs and priorities. You need to work out what your poker goals are and what risks you are prepared to take. Just ensure that you are constantly mindful of those snippets from the Poker Mindset that we discussed earlier in the chapter:

1. Understand and accept that poker is a game of high variance.
2. Play for the long term.
3. Leave your ego at the door.

Remember what we said earlier: It is not only the actual risk of losing your bankroll, but also the fear of losing your bankroll that we need to contend with. Use the Poker Mindset and proper bankroll management to help eliminate that fear, and your poker game will be much better for it.

7.7. Chapter Review

❑ 7.1. The Biggest Mistake in Poker
- Good bankroll management is one of the most important skills you will learn when playing poker. In fact, poor bankroll management could be considered the biggest mistake in poker.
- Bankroll management is simply the practice of ensuring that you have enough money to play poker for the long term.
- It is not only the actual risk of losing your bankroll, but also the fear of losing your bankroll that we need to contend with.
- If the fear of going broke is preying on your mind, then this is likely to lead to bad decisions at the table.

❑ 7.2. Determining Your Bankroll Requirements
- Your base level for limit poker is 300 big bets and for big-bet poker 20 buy-ins. Your base level for tournaments should be about 75 buy-ins.
- These guidelines should be modified according to your specific circumstances and games you play.

❑ 7.3. Why Do Players Go Wrong?

- Even a player who has learned to play poker well may manage his bankroll badly for many reasons.
  - Bankroll recommendations seem very conservative
  - Players overestimate their own ability
  - The allure of the higher limits
  - Bad habits from the lower limits
  - Acting foolishly when under pressure

❑ 7.4. Moving Up Limits

- There is no rule that you have to move up when you have the bankroll for the next limit. Some reasons for not moving up a limit as soon as you can include:
  - You haven't mastered your current limit
  - You don't think you can beat the new limit
  - You are scared by the higher nominal swings
- The Peter Principle of Poker: Poker rooms contain a lot of former winning players who have advanced to a limit that they cannot beat.

❑ 7.5. Moving Down Limits

- If you are running badly to a point where you no longer have a sufficient bankroll for your current limit, then you should drop down a limit.
- Most players hate dropping down limits as they think it represents a step backwards in their poker career. Consciously or otherwise, it is considered a defeat or an admission of failure, and their ego does not like it.
- Buffer zones help prevent cheating on your bankroll requirements, by incorporating some downward inertia into your bankroll plans.

❑ 7.6. Cashing-out Strategies

- If, when, and how you should cash out is not clear-cut because of conflicting interests:
  - On one hand, you would like to keep growing your bankroll so that you can play at higher and higher limits and see potentially bigger wins in cash terms.
  - On the other hand, there is no point in doing this if you never get to reap the rewards of your labors.
- Look out for the following errors when you consider cashing out:
  - Cashing out more than you make each month on average.
  - Cashing out meaningless amounts.
  - Never cashing out (you are probably missing the point of poker if you never cash out).
  - Falling victim to the Peter Principle of Poker.
  - Not incorporating cashing out into your bankroll strategy.

Chapter 8

Into the Minds of Your Opponents

"Poker is not a game of cards, it's a game of people." –
Anonymous

There are two sides to poker psychology. The first is mastering your own Poker Mindset — your emotions and thought processes — to play the best poker you can as often as possible. This is the more important side of poker psychology, as you will always struggle to be a winning player if you are unable to conquer your own demons first.

The other side to poker psychology is understanding how your opponents think and act. Up to now, this book has focused on mastering your own emotional control. This chapter takes the next step by crossing over the boundary to look at the subject of reading and understanding your opponents. We have looked at many topics in relation to our own play, so it only makes sense to cross over and look at them with respect to our opponents.

Fortunately, everything you have learned so far will help a great deal in understanding your opponents better. By understanding the obstacles in achieving the correct Poker Mindset, you not only understand what you need to do to better manage your emotions, but now you'll also understand the obstacles that your opponents face. By knowing what causes your opponents to do the things they do, you will be better prepared to recognize the various states of mind your opponents exhibit.

8.1. The Importance of Observation

Great poker players will tell you that they play the player, not the cards. Some top players have boasted that they could win without even looking at their cards.[53] One of the most important things you must do at the poker table is continually study your opponents to learn whatever you can about how they play and how they react to particular situations.

Some players do not take any notice of their opponents at all. Weak or novice players generally do not recognize the importance of studying their opponents, failing to look beyond their own cards when deciding what to do. This in itself may not be surprising. More surprising is that better players can sometimes be guilty of failing to study their opponents thoroughly. This may be for a number of reasons, such as:

1. They are too lazy.
2. They are playing multiple tables on the Internet.
3. They hold their opponents in so much contempt that they do not consider it worth their time to analyze their play individually, instead opting to use loosely fitting labels such as "fish" or "idiot."
4. They too often let things such as TV, talking with their opponents, or any of the many distractions that might occur while playing at home on the Internet interfere with their game.

These players might be able to scrape a profit at the tables but will never fulfill their potential. They will eventually hit a wall when they progress to higher limits, where playing your opponent becomes more important.

You are much more likely to make good decisions at the poker table if you do study your opponents and know how to use that information. Simple observation, however, will only take you so far. The quality

---

[53] As long as their opponents did not know they were not looking at their cards.

of your decisions will naturally depend upon the quality of your observations. There is a lot of difference between making a very general, broad observation about a player, and taking detailed notes (either mental notes or written notes) about how he plays specific hands and holdings.

For example, describing a player as "loose" is only vaguely useful. A more helpful description might be, "He is loose pre-flop and on the flop, but plays correctly more often on the turn when the bets get bigger." An even better observation might be "He plays too many weak suited hands pre-flop and will call the flop with any over card. He often lets his weak hands go on the turn when the bets are bigger, but will still continue with second pair for one bet, even on a scary board."

The more information you have about an opponent and the more specific it is, the better.

Although this statement might seem obvious on the surface, it is important to recognize that observation is a never-ending process. There is no time for rest. Many players are happy with general observations and fail to take it to the next level. In reality, you should constantly be making observations about your opponents. Continuous observation is the key to advancing your game to the next level.

Action Point: The next time you play poker, pay special attention to one player at random. Every time you see something about the way he plays, no matter how mundane, write it down. Include what hands he showed down and how he bet them, how he acted with strong and weak hands, and whether he bluffed or slow-played at all. Obviously, you won't be able to keep track of everything for every opponent, but by tracking one particular opponent, it will become clear just how much can be learned through careful observation.

Spotting changes

First impressions are useful, but be wary of placing too much faith in your initial observations of a player. Another destructive facet of the human psyche is that once a person has formed an opinion about something, he will embrace evidence that supports that opinion and disregard evidence that contradicts it. In poker terms, he will put a label on a player and then stubbornly stick to that label despite mounting evidence to the contrary.

For example, you play a session with a player and notice that he is playing very loosely, showing down some very questionable hands. Sometime in the future you are delighted to see that player again. You sit in the perfect seat to his left and proceed to value bet and isolate him relentlessly, hoping to capitalize on your superior starting hands. However, you are constantly frustrated when he shows down better hands than you. When you have A-J, he has A-Q; when you have A-T, he has TT. You walk away wondering what happened.

What happened is that the player wasn't playing as loose as in the previous session. You failed to notice this because you had already labeled the player as loose and were ignoring the mounting evidence to the contrary. There are a number of possible explanations for his change in behavior:

- The first time you played with him, he was on tilt.
- His "loose" play in the first session was in fact his own attempts to adjust to the play of another wild player.
- He improved his game since your previous meeting.

Alternatively, maybe he didn't change his play at all. It's possible your opponent is still a loose player and just got a string of good hands during your second meeting, but the more likely scenario is that something indeed was different with his play. The point is that you have to constantly monitor a player to fine-tune your knowledge of his play. This includes analyzing whether your first impressions were in fact correct or whether they were actually misleading. In fact, your analysis of even the most straightforward player should never be considered complete.

8.2. Categorizing Your Opponents

The longer you play against a particular opponent, the clearer the picture becomes of that player's overall game. However, even after playing a thousand hands against the same player, you can't possibly expect to know everything about the way he plays, even if he plays relatively straightforwardly.

For most opponents you will face on a day-to-day basis, you will in fact have far less than a thousand hands on which to make your evaluation. Instead, you will need to invoke a certain degree of stereotyping and assumption, based on what you *do* know. Traditionally, poker players like to measure their opponents against established benchmarks such as:

- How many hands they play (i.e., how "loose" they are).
- How often they raise as opposed to call (i.e., how "aggressive" they are)
- How often they misrepresent their hand (i.e., how "tricky" or "deceptive" they are).

When taken together, these three measures will give you a reasonable framework on which to base your decisions. You could label a player as Tight-Passive-Straightforward, Loose-Aggressive-Deceptive, or any other permutation, and then add further details about his game as you discover them.[54]

The above method of notation is the standard method that poker players use to categorize players, but to truly understand your opponent, you will need to go deeper than that. By observing how tight, aggressive,

---

[54] Online players may have additional tools available to them. Software is available that allows you to keep a large database of hand histories and request statistical information about your opponents. Naturally, this makes categorizing your opponents a lot easier.

or deceptive a player is, all you are really seeing is how certain traits of that player are manifesting themselves through his play. To truly get into the mind of your opponents, you need to understand not only how they act in certain situations, but also *why* they act the way they do.

For example, let's say you know three players whom you categorize as Loose-Aggressive-Deceptive. They play a lot of pots, raise a lot, and try to mislead you whenever possible. That description does not mean that these three players all play the same way. In fact, they may all be very different in their motives.

Player A might be a gambler. He plays a lot of hands and raises a lot because he craves action. He doesn't care about pot odds or anything like that. He just wants to get his money in the middle. He will make outrageous bluffs on the off chance they will work, and will call down or raise with slim draws hoping to hit a big payday.

Player B might be a bully. He bets and raises a lot because he likes to be in charge of the table. He wants other players to be scared of him, and he wants to be the alpha male at the table. He is trying to win, but only on his own terms.

Player C might be a speculative player. He is trying to win money by playing lots of hands and is trying to outplay his opponents after the flop. He will push his hand hard if he thinks he is ahead and will bluff at a pot if he thinks it might work. If he thinks he is behind with little chance of catching up, he will fold.

Of course, observing whether a player is loose, tight, aggressive, passive, straightforward, or tricky is important, but you need to go beyond that. In the following sections, we look at additional ways to categorize your opponents. First, we find out how to determine what *type* of player your opponent is and how this will influence his decisions at the table. We then look at the levels on which your opponent is thinking, which will help determine your best strategy for beating him.

By the end of this chapter, you will have three different tools with which to evaluate your opponents. You will be able to determine:

1. How they play in terms of looseness, aggression, and trickiness.
2. What type of player they are.
3. What level they think on.

Taken together, these three observations will give you a powerful advantage at the table.

8.3. Different Types of Players

In the previous section, we gave the example of three players who have a similar style but whose drives and motives, and hence their precise betting patterns, are very different. One of the first things you should try to determine is the type of opponent you are facing. Sometimes you can generate an idea before even playing a hand! The main way of determining the type of player you face is through analyzing his betting patterns, but you can also glean clues from other places such as:

Appearance – A player's age, appearance, and attire can give you an indication of the type of player he might be.

Mannerisms – How does he act at the table? Does he appear confident or nervous? Does he seem uncertain of the rules or protocols?

What He Says – Some players will give away huge clues about the type of player they are by what they say. This applies to both comments about the game and non-poker-related comments that give you a clue as to the type of person they might be.[55]

---

[55] Note that this is the only one of the three that is available to Internet players. Watch that chat box closely.

After a while, you will start to see players not only as the sum of their playing characteristics but as fully rounded people. You will begin to categorize them not only by how they play but also by how they think. In the last section, we observed three of these categories: the gambler, the bully, and the speculative player. The following are some examples of the types of players you might meet at the poker table, along with tips on how to identify them and an idea of how they might play. This list is by no means exhaustive. After a while, you will start to notice other stereotypes, too.

The newbie

New players will be trying to find their feet in the game. They will make the plays that they think are right, but these will not usually be based on conventional poker theory. Generally, they will play very loosely and passively because this is how most players instinctively like to play. New players will have a lot to take in, and so their play will usually lack imagination and deception. Their motives are to learn the game and have fun without losing too much money.

New players are usually quite easy to identify. They will often look confused and/or nervous and will probably have to ask the dealer a lot of questions. If you are in a casino in a tourist resort like Las Vegas or Los Angeles, you might notice tell-tale signs of a tourist wanting to "try out" poker, such as a camera or gift-shop bags.

The casual player

Casual players make up a large proportion of the poker-playing population, and so appearance-wise at least, they are difficult to stereotype. The best way to identify casual players is by their demeanor and playing style. They will know how to play the game and will not normally appear nervous. They play the game for fun, as evidenced by their words and actions.

The catch is that most casual players don't *think* they only play for fun. In fact, most of them will say they play for money. In reality, though, they are almost all long-term losers because they don't play the game the way it should be played. They want to win, but only on their terms. Like the newbies, casual players tend to play too loosely and too passively, because that is the way they *want* to play.

The gambler

Gamblers play neither for fun nor to win in the classic sense (although both elements are a factor). They play because they enjoy the buzz of gambling; they want to get their money in the pot and then see if they've won. For this reason, they are nearly always loose, and often aggressive, too. They might or might not be deceptive.

Gamblers are generally very focused and single-minded while playing the game. When they run out of chips, they will often reload without skipping a beat. They don't tend to get mad when they lose, because they are used to it; deep down, winning isn't that important to them.

The rock

The rock is a pedestrian and predictable opponent. He will play in a very tight, passive, and straightforward style that allows him to lose his money very slowly or maybe even eek out a profit in certain games. If he raises, then he will nearly always have a very good hand.

Rocks play in a style that is not at all fun to play, but then again, they usually aren't playing for fun. Most are playing either to pass the time (often the case with retired players) or to extract a small profit from a game that contains a number of weak players. You can normally identify rocks as quiet players who blend into the background. In fact, you will hardly notice they are at the table at all. Even on the rare occasion when they enter a pot, they will normally do so timidly, with a limp.

The bully

The bully's main motivation is to be in charge of the table. He wants to win, but more pressingly, he wants to play in a style that will make other players fear him. His ego, rather than good poker sense, tends to make his decisions. Bullies generally play a loose, aggressive style, not only because this is the style most likely to intimidate other players, but also because it matches their personality somewhat.

Spotting the bully is quite easy. He is usually loud, often obnoxious, and will try to intimidate his opponents both with words and body language. When the bully loses a big pot, he will handle it badly, blaming his opponent's play, the dealer, the deck, or anything else in an attempt to heal his damaged ego.

The developing player

When a new player sets off on the road to becoming a winning player, he will usually go through several stages before he learns all the intricacies of the game. He is keen and pays close attention to the game, but his play is raw and he will make mistakes (and often beat himself up over them).

The developing player's game may go through a number of phases during this period, and so it can be difficult to predict how he will play. He will often get stuck in a tight-passive stage for a while, where he has learned to play tight but has not yet learned the full value of playing aggressively (or does not have the confidence to).

The speculative player

Speculative players play to win but do not have the discipline to play a tight-aggressive style, so they try to win with a loose-aggressive one instead. They can be quite dangerous to play against because they are difficult to put on a hand and generally play well post-flop. Sometimes they are winners, but often they cannot play well enough to overcome the trash hands they are starting with.

Speculative players are often the center of attention at the table — not because they want to be (unlike the bully), but because their style of play puts them in the thick of the action a lot. Some players will be scared of them, some scornful, while the better players will be trying to adapt their game to compensate. Speculative players are usually younger players.

The nit

The word "nit" has been used to describe a lot of different players over the years, but most commonly refers to a tight player who is generally unfriendly and pedantic. Nits are usually marginal winners who are very careful about the games they play and will never leave their comfort zone. Although they are rarely big winners, they do play to win rather than just for fun.

Nits are generally quite easy to identify. Sometimes they are quiet and sullen, while other times they take on the role of "table professor," telling other players what they are doing wrong. They are often unable to adapt to loose-aggressive players and are uncomfortable in their presence. In many ways, nits resemble rocks, but they are not always passive and predictable, and are usually more concerned about things like game selection. Nits are usually disliked by the other regular players.

The robot

Robots are winning players who play a generally good game of poker. They do not win as much as they could because they tend to play very mechanically, without paying as much attention to the game as they should. This is sometimes because they don't enjoy the game that much, sometimes because they are lazy, and sometimes because they treat poker more like a job and simply go through the motions.

Robots are extremely common online. They will often play up to eight tables at once, without really concentrating very hard on any of them individually. They can also be found in a live casino, where they will play quite well but look disinterested in the game. Robots tend to play a tight-aggressive style but can be fairly predictable. They rely on their superior hand selection and knowledge of the game to win money from weaker players.

The shark

The shark is a strong player who not only plays good poker but also studies the particulars of the game he is in and adapts accordingly. The shark wants to make money, plain and simple. He probably enjoys the game, too, but his primary motivation is always making the decision that gives him the best expectation.

To spot a shark, look for a player playing calmly and confidently, usually with a tight-aggressive style.[56] His opponents will envy, idolize, dislike, suck up to, and fear him in equal measure. Sometimes sharks go in disguise, though. They might deliberately style themselves to look like a new player, a casual player, or a gambler. If a player's appearance is telling you one thing and his play is telling you another, always believe his play.[57]

> Action Point: Think about some of your regular opponents. Try to determine in which of the above ten categories they each belong. Are there any players who seem to belong in multiple categories or in none of them?

Not all players fall nicely within these ten categories. Sometimes you will meet players who seem to be a hybrid of more than one type. For example, you might meet a new player who has good card instincts and plays more like a speculative player than a new player. Alternatively, you might play with a shark who acts like a bully toward his opponents. Sometimes you will meet a player who doesn't seem to fit into any of these categories at all.

The important thing is not that you squeeze every opponent into a category, but that you think about what each player's motivations are. If you know why a player is playing and what he might be thinking, then this information can go a long way toward interpreting his actions and predicting future ones.[58]

---

[56] Although, they may adopt a different style if the situation warrants it, such as in a short-handed game.

[57] Sharks play well, but not all of them fully embrace the Poker Mindset. You might find sharks who are good players but go on tilt easily or become obsessed with downswings.

[58] For more discussion on labeling players, we recommend *The Psychology of Poker* by Alan Schoonmaker.

8.4. Getting into Your Opponents' Heads

At the lower limits, against weak players, you might be able to make money by playing poker on autopilot, making textbook moves similar to that of a robot. At higher limits, you generally will need at least a rudimentary understanding of why your individual opponents make certain plays and how they might respond to your own actions.

A costly mistake that many players make is that of projection: assuming that our opponents think the way we think.

Consciously or otherwise, we will project our own logic and thought process onto our opponents, even though we have no evidence to assume they think the same way we do. In fact, we might do this even when we have evidence to the contrary.

For example, consider a hand from a no-limit tournament as seen from the point of view of a decent player whom we will call Martin. His opponent in this hand is a weak player named Simon. Martin has a slightly above-average stack, while Simon's is below average but not yet dangerously low.

Martin open raises from the cutoff with a standard raise holding Q-T suited, and Simon calls from the big blind. The flop comes 9-8-4 rainbow, giving Martin a gutshot straight draw and two overcards. Simon opens with a bet about half the size of the pot. Martin concludes that Simon is making a probing bet with a weak made hand in order to see where he stands, probably holding an 8 or a 9. Martin decides he is probably behind but is also likely to have a lot of outs and good implied odds, so he calls.

The turn is a 7, which gives Martin an open-ended straight draw, but more important, probably hasn't helped Simon. He does not think that Simon's play so far indicates the possibility of J-T, two pair or a set. Simon makes a weak-looking bet of about a third of the pot, which

202 **The Poker Mindset: Essential Attitudes for Poker Success**

Martin reads as a scared bet. He decides that the best play would be to make a large raise. He reasons that Simon wouldn't risk his entire tournament life with a weak hand on a scary board, and would probably give Martin credit for a straight, set or overpair. If he had read the situation wrongly and Simon did have a set or two pair, he would still have eight outs to the straight.

Martin re-raised about twice the size of the pot, a raise large enough that Simon would not have the odds to chase a straight or a flush. Simon thought for about 10 seconds and then called. The river was a blank, an off-suit deuce, and Simon checked. Simon was now short-stacked and pot-committed. Martin felt there was no chance he could bet Simon out of the pot, so he checked behind. Simon showed Q-9 and took down the pot with his pair of nines. "How could he possibly call that turn raise," Martin muttered to his neighbor as the next hand was dealt.

Now let's look at the same hand from Simon's point of view. He is a casual player who plays poker mainly for fun. He plays in this tournament when he has $50 to spare, hoping that one day he will get lucky and have a big payday. He tries to play good poker, but lacks the understanding or experience to make the right plays.

In this hand, he is dealt Q-9 in the big blind. When Martin raises and everyone else folds, he considers that he has two big cards and so can play. He has already paid his big blind, so it would be a shame to fold this reasonable-looking hand without even seeing the flop. The flop comes 9-8-4, which looks like a great flop to Simon. He has top pair and decides to bet. He doesn't really look at how much he's betting and simply grabs a few chips from his stack. Martin calls.

A seven comes on turn, which means Simon still has top pair. He bets some more chips and then sees Martin make a big raise. Simon doesn't really know what Martin has and still likes his top pair, so he calls. Simon checks the river with the intention of calling the rest of his chips if Martin bets again. Martin checks, and Simon is delighted to win such a big pot.

Do you see where Martin went wrong in this hand? He automatically assumed that Simon thought in the same way he did. He pictured what he would do in Simon's position and then projected that picture onto Simon, who in reality wasn't thinking terribly hard at all and certainly wasn't clever enough to make the "correct laydown" on the turn. In effect, Martin out-thought himself, making a sophisticated play that went completely over his opponent's head.

Assuming your opponent thinks the way you do is a significant mistake, and one that you should be especially wary of when playing against weak opposition. Instead of thinking about what you would do in a particular situation, consider what you know about your opponent and try and imagine what he would do. It seems obvious, but it is easy to forget in the heat of battle.

This is why it is so useful to study your opponent to try to understand what type of player and person he is. It makes good decision-making far easier when crunch time comes. For example, let's say you are playing limit Hold'em and have a busted draw on the river. You know there is no chance that you have the best hand, and your only decision is whether you should bluff at the pot. From the betting so far, you put your opponent on a weak made hand, such as a low pair. One factor in your favor is that the river was a scare card. It was an over card to the board (an ace), which also completed a possible flush. Let's look at how you might play the river against the players described in the previous section.

The new player – Against new players, you wouldn't bet at this pot, because the chance of them folding for one bet on the river is minuscule. They will simply be playing their own hand and will probably not even see what you are trying to represent.

The casual player – Similarly, the casual player is also unlikely to fold on the river for one bet. Even if he is sure he is beaten, he will call just to "look at what you had" or to "see how I am beat."

The gambler – The gambler certainly isn't folding. He just wants to get all his money in and see if he has won; having come this far, he is hardly going to fold.

The rock – Against the rock, a bet might well work. Rocks tend to assume the worst in the face of adversity. If you bet and they have a weak hand, then they may well let it go. They won't fold every time, but then again they only have to fold a small portion of the time for the bet to be profitable.

The bully – The bully would definitely not fold in this situation. It would look like weakness, and his ego would not allow it. In fact, he may even see your bet as an attempt to get one over on him, and decide to raise.

The developing player – Bluffing is worth a shot against the developing player because he may not realize that this is a good situation in which to bluff. He will still have some large leaks in his game, and one common leak is folding too often on the river.

The speculative player – Speculative players tend to play quite well after the flop. It may be worth a shot if your betting so far is consistent with having an ace or a flush draw; otherwise, save your money

The nit – It is definitely worth taking a shot against the nit. Nits pride themselves on being good players. Give them the chance to make a "good laydown," then listen to them lecture the table about how they put you on an ace all along and you got lucky.

The robot – The robot is probably not concentrating fully on the game. All he will see is a player betting on the river when he holds a weak hand. He is quite likely to give it up without really thinking the situation through. Make the bet.

The shark – The shark will immediately see the threat that the river card introduces, but on the other hand, he will also see that this is a good spot for a bluff. It is difficult to bluff a shark when he is getting good pot odds on a call. You should only make a bet here if your play has been consistent with having an ace or a flush draw *and* you have a table image that makes him consider it unlikely that you would bluff.

This kind of thinking will not apply to every decision you make, but it probably applies to more than you imagine. The above example shows how you might use your knowledge of a player to predict his actions. You might also use similar thinking to try to interpret what one of his actions means. For example, if you are raised on the turn, then this may mean very different things depending on whom you are up against.

What is important is that you understand the motivations of each type of player. For example, a casual player wants to have fun, a developing player wants to learn, a bully wants to be feared, a shark or robot wants to win, and a rock is generally more concerned with not losing. In any situation, think about how that player might be trying to accomplish these goals.

Labels such as "tight passive" are less helpful. No player in the history of poker has ever made a decision by thinking, "I'm tight passive, so I will check." Look beyond the symptoms and find what facet of his personality causes a player to act tight passive in the first place. Perhaps the same facet causes him to act completely different in another situation.

8.5. Levels of Thinking

We have already discussed two ways of evaluating your opponent. The first is the traditional method of rating your opponent on poker variables such as looseness, aggression, and deceptiveness. The second is categorizing your opponents by their personality and motives. Together, these two methods provide a very powerful way of reading your opponent. In this section, we introduce a third method, which can make your evaluation even more powerful.

When playing a poker hand, there are a number of different levels on which you can think, each more involved and complex than the last.

Level 0 – What hand do you have? Many poker theorists don't even consider this a level of thinking at all,[59] because your cards and the community cards are right there in front of you. A player thinking at level 0 is only focused on the strength of his hand and doesn't consider what his opponent has or what he is thinking.

Level 1 – What hand might your opponent have? If you are thinking at level 1, you are considering your opponent's possible holdings and acting accordingly.

Level 2 – What does your opponent think you have? We are now entering the more complex levels of poker analysis. Level 2 thinking is the process of looking at your own betting, style, and image to see what conclusions your opponent might draw as a result, and hence what his betting might mean.

Level 3 – What does your opponent think that you think he has? At this level, you are evaluating your opponent's betting based on how you think he might be responding to your betting.

Level 3 is the highest level of thinking that is usually defined, but actually the levels are never-ending. Level 4 would be what does your opponent think that you think that he thinks you have, and so on.

It might appear that you should try to think at as high a level as possible, but this is actually not the case. Remember the hand between Martin and Simon? Martin was thinking on level 2, trying to make a play on the basis of what his opponent would think he had. Unfortunately for Martin, Simon wasn't even thinking about what Martin might hold. Simon was thinking at level 0.

In this hand, Martin was thinking a level too high. There is no point in thinking two or more levels above your opponent, because these

---

[59] Hence why it is level 0, not level 1.

levels assume a degree of analysis from your opponent that isn't there. The level you should be thinking at is entirely dependent on what level your opponent is thinking at. Ideally, you want to be thinking at one level, *and only one level,* above your opponent.

If your opponent is thinking at level 0, then you want to be at level 1. He is only thinking about his own hand, so you need to try to determine what his hand is through his betting. There is no point in bluffing a scare card or slow-playing a big hand because your opponent is not thinking about what you might have; he is only considering his own hand.

If your opponent is thinking at level 1, then you want to be at level 2. He is trying to work out what hand you might hold, so you want to determine what he thinks you have and hence what his bets mean. Remember that if an opponent is adopting level 1 thinking, his bets don't always mean what they appear to mean. For example, if he puts you on a weak hand, he may bet even if his own hand is weak to induce a fold. However, he won't be considering what hand you put him on and so won't try a sophisticated play like raising a flush card on the river.

If your opponent is thinking at level 2, then you want to be at level 3. He is trying to decipher your bets based on what hand he thinks you put him on. Therefore, you need to go one stage further and respond to his bets based on the fact that he is thinking this way. Ironically, in some situations, you can outfox a level 2 player by returning to level 0 thinking and just betting your hand.

If you are two or more levels ahead of your opponent, then you have no advantage. In fact, you may actually be at a disadvantage. It is therefore important that you estimate as closely as possible your opponent's level of thinking.

One difficulty with this is that most players tend to think at different levels at different times. When a player is in a familiar situation, he is more likely to think at a higher level than usual. For example, when many players flop a monster (such as a set, full house, straight, or flush), they will simply check and call the flop in the hope of drawing their opponents into losing more money on later streets. This is effectively level 2 thinking, because they are trying to manipulate what their opponents think they have. However, when faced with a difficult and unfamiliar situation, the same players will just revert to the level 0 or 1 thinking with which they are more familiar.

In addition, while you might know the level of your opponent's thinking, you might have no idea how clearly he is thinking and how he is applying that knowledge. For example, a casual player may put you on a hand that beats his (level 1 thinking), but then calls you down anyway because he hates folding and thus not being able to see if he was right in his assessment.

We now have three tools that we can use to categorize our opponents:

1. What is their general playing style? How loose, aggressive, and deceptive are they?
2. What type of player are they and how do their primary motivations for playing influence their decision-making?
3. On what level do they think?

Each of these considerations has its own limitations, but when taken together, they can be a powerful way to enable you to get inside the minds of your opponents. If we can understand the reasons why opponents think the way they do, and therefore act in certain ways, we can take our understanding of our opponents to new levels.

Action Point: Go back to the detailed notes about one particular player that you made in the earlier action point. Try to build a profile of that player using the above three tools. Then go back and start again with a different player.

8.6. Chapter Review

❑ 8.1. The Importance of Observation

- One of the most important things you must do at the poker table is continually study your opponents to learn whatever you can about how they play and how they react to particular situations.
- The quality of your decisions will naturally depend upon the quality of your observations.
- The more information you have about an opponent and the more specific it is, the better.
- First impressions are useful, but be wary of placing too much faith in your initial observations of a player.

❑ 8.2. Categorizing Your Opponents

- Traditionally, poker players like to measure their opponents against established benchmarks such as:
  - How many hands they play (i.e., how "loose" they are).
  - How often they raise as opposed to call (i.e., how "aggressive" they are).
  - How often they misrepresent their hand (i.e., how "tricky" or "deceptive" they are).
- To truly get into the mind of your opponents, you need to understand not only how they act in certain situations, but also *why* they act the way they do.

❑ 8.3. Different Types of Players

- The main way of determining the type of player you face is through analyzing his betting patterns, but you can also glean clues from other places such as appearance, mannerisms, and what he says.
- If you know why a player is playing and what he might be thinking, then this information can go a long way toward interpreting his actions and predicting future ones.

❑ 8.4. Getting into Your Opponents' Heads

- A costly mistake that many players make is that of projection: assuming that our opponents think the way we think.
- Instead of thinking about what you would do in a particular situation, consider what you know about your opponent and try and imagine what *he* would do.
- What is important is that you understand the motivations of each type of player. In any situation, think about how that player might be trying to accomplish these goals.

❑ 8.5. Levels of Thinking

- When playing a poker hand, there are a number of different levels on which you can think, each more involved and complex than the last.
  - Level 0 – What hand do you have?
  - Level 1 – What hand might your opponent have?
  - Level 2 – What does your opponent think you have?
  - Level 3 – What does your opponent think that you think he has?
- Ideally, you want to be thinking at one level, *and only one level,* above your opponent.
- We now have three tools that we can use to categorize our opponents:
  1. What is their general playing style? How loose, aggressive, and deceptive are they?
  2. What type of player are they and how do their primary motivations for playing influence their decision-making?
  3. On what level do they think?

Chapter 9

Advanced Topics

"Once you start thinking you have nothing left to learn, you have everything to learn." – Steve Badger

The main body of this book is complete. You now have the information you need to establish the correct emotional, psychological, and behavioral approach to playing poker. Plus, you have the weapons you need to conquer the greatest enemy you will face at the poker table: yourself. In this chapter, we will tie up loose ends and discuss some areas of poker psychology that don't quite fit elsewhere but are important nonetheless.

9.1. When to Quit

Everyone knows the popular saying "Quit while you're ahead." You'll hear it from numerous tourists in Vegas playing the slots, blackjack, and craps. This is actually good advice for those players as they are destined to lose their winnings if they play long enough in games with negative expectation.

Poker is different. For winning players, poker has a positive expectation whenever they sit down at the table. For losing players, it is like playing slots or blackjack; they will eventually lose all of their money if they play long enough. For both winning and losing players, however, the question still remains: "When should you quit a session?"

Determining the best time to quit a session is a topic often debated among poker players. Should you try to quit while you are ahead, before you have a chance to give back your winnings? Alternatively, should you quit when you're behind to make sure you don't lose any more? What other signs should you look for that will tell you it's time to end your session?

From a poker point of view, there are only two reasons why you ever need to end your session:

1. You are no longer playing your best (i.e., you are on tilt).

It is a bad idea to carry on playing when you are on tilt, even if you still think that you have an edge in the game. We discussed the reasons for this in chapter 6, but in case you need a reminder, here is a summary of the reasons:

1. You are probably overestimating your edge.
2. You may not realize how badly you are tilting.
3. Your game may deteriorate further.

2. You are unable to beat the game (or find another within your bankroll that you can).

This second reason to quit speaks for itself. If you don't have an edge in the game, then why bother playing? Come back another time when you *can* find a game where you have an edge.[60] As an aside, one thing you should never be tempted to do is to play above your bankroll because you see what looks like a juicy game at that limit while there are none at yours. Reread chapter 7 if you don't understand the reasoning behind this.

These are the only two poker-related reasons why you should end your session. Of course, you will frequently quit for other reasons

---

[60] For the Internet player, this is almost never an issue. There are so many sites and so many tables that you are almost certain to find a good game.

completely unrelated to poker, such as being hungry or tired, having to meet someone or be somewhere else, or wanting to watch your favorite TV program. Leaving for any of these reasons is perfectly fine; we are certainly not here to instruct you on how to prioritize your life. In fact, you *should* have other things to do with your life besides playing poker.[61]

But what about those reasons we mentioned at the start of this section? Should you quit because you are ahead or because you are behind? Do these reasons have any merit at all? Generally speaking, they do not. There is absolutely no point in quitting because you are winning, and very little point in quitting purely because you are behind. To understand why, we need to distance ourselves from the idea of a "session." Although the results of an individual session seem important, they are actually of no real importance at all.

Try to imagine every hand of poker you have ever played, and every hand you will play in the future, as one big long session. Because we are human and need to eat, sleep, go to work, and do other things, we have to take breaks from this big long session. However, when we return to the table, we pick up where we left off. Sure, our opponents will have changed, the dealer will be different, and maybe we'll even be in a totally different casino. But we are still playing the same game, putting those same chips on the line.

If you quit because you're ahead or behind, then you are really just delaying the results of your next hand until your next session. For example, you win 20 big bets in a session and you leave the table so as not to lose again. But what are you achieving exactly? You are not protecting those 20 big bets in any way, because you will have to put some of them at risk during the next hand. It doesn't matter whether that next hand is in 30 seconds' time or next week; you still risk losing it (unless, of course, you plan on quitting poker forever). The same reasoning applies to a losing session. You don't want to lose any more, but at some point you are going to return to the table and risk losing more anyway, so why not now?

---

[61] See chapter 10 for more on this.

Think back to that one long session again. We will make it a bit more manageable by just looking at the results from one week rather than a lifetime. Imagine a line graph where your winnings are plotted against the number of hands you played. The graph will go up and down because poker is a high-variance game, and may look something like this in a particular week.

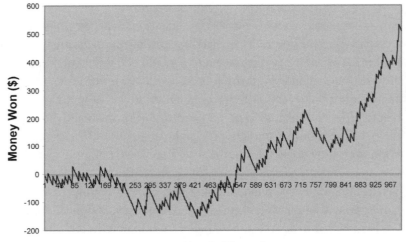

Hands Played

This represents 1,000 hands played over the course of a week. Let's now assume that we played 200 hands per night for five nights and mark on the graph where these five sessions ended.

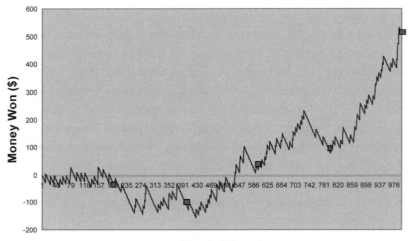

Hands Played

Do you see what difference it makes where the sessions ended? That's right, absolutely none! You had two losing sessions followed by three winning sessions, but these points are arbitrary. You could quite easily rearrange those dots so you had only one losing session, or three, or even none. Looking at the week as a whole, it makes absolutely no difference; you still finish with the same result (a net win of around $500).

Hopefully, this illustrates the reason why quitting because you are ahead or behind is futile. If you win those 20 big bets and carry on playing, then there is a chance you will lose them again. There is also a chance you will win more. Most important, if you do quit, then you will be faced with exactly the same issue when you next sit down at the table. The key lesson to be learned here is:

Don't look at each session as a fresh start; instead, look at each hand as a fresh start, not to be influenced by any hands that have come before it.

Stop-loss limits

Many advanced players recommend "stop-loss" limits when you are playing poker. A stop-loss limit is where you set a sum in advance, say, 30 big bets in limit Hold'em, at which you will quit the session if you lose that much. This advice contradicts what we have just stated: There is no reason to quit as long as you are playing your best and can beat the game. Which piece of advice is correct?

Both are correct in a sense. While it is entirely true that there is no logic in quitting solely because you are behind, stop-loss limits can be a good idea for other reasons. This is explained by going back to the two valid poker-related reasons for quitting a session:

1. You are no longer playing your best.
2. You are unable to beat the game.

Losing a certain sum of money in a session may be a sign that you are no longer playing your best or that you are in fact unable to beat the game.

For many players, stop-loss limits can be beneficial so that you can take stock of the situation. Think back to the hands you lost money on and see if you can understand why you lost. It might be that you just took a lot of bad beats or didn't get any cards, in which case there is nothing to worry about. Alternatively, it might be that your game was off or you were being outplayed.

In addition, losing a lot of money in a session is a common trigger for tilt. Your play may deteriorate as you become obsessed with your losses, or lament bad beats or bad cards. You might also try too hard to win that money back, which, as we discussed in chapter 6, is a sure-fire way to put yourself on tilt by playing too loosely or by playing too long when you are tired.

Ideally, we would constantly maintain the perfect Poker Mindset. We would always play our best poker, and we could say that a loss is just a reality of poker variance. Therefore, there would be no reason to quit when we were behind in a session. In reality, it is difficult to achieve the perfect Poker Mindset, and it is important to understand and acknowledge our own limitations. It is difficult to play our best poker 100% of the time. Rarely is a player completely unaffected by losses. If you are unable to reach the stage where you accept losses or are indifferent to them, then setting stop-loss limits is a good idea. There is no shame in leaving a good game if you are on tilt, as you will probably lose even more money if you continue to play.

9.2. What about Upswings?

We spent an entire chapter discussing how to deal with a downswing, but no time at all looking at the flip side of variance. Should we not spend the same time discussing the psychology of being on an upswing?

Some players would say there is no need. When you think about it, no player needs to be told how to deal with an upswing. You just carry on playing and raking in the money, right? Well, in a way, yes. Dealing with an upswing is certainly far easier than dealing with a downswing, which is why we didn't feel the need to discuss it in chapter 5. Generally, there is less to say regarding upswings because:

There is no vicious circle – As discussed, the main problem with downswings is that they feed upon themselves. In other words, the worse you play, the worse your results, which can put you even further on tilt and so on. There is no such vicious circle when on an upswing.[62] In fact, if there were, we would love to know about it!

Tilt is less likely – Players are considerably less likely to go on tilt when running well than when running badly. They will not be playing scared nor be desperate to get back even. Feelings of happiness and confidence are less conducive to tilt than those of depression and self-doubt.

No desire to make changes – While a player on a downswing will want to make changes to his game, a player on an upswing will have no such wish. This eliminates (or at least severely reduces) the chance that the player will make a rash, ill-advised change.

Despite the above, there are still dangers associated with being on an upswing; they are just less severe than those you face when on a downswing. The most common pitfalls when you are running well can be summarized as follows:

---

[62] However, there are some players who can build on their wins. They become more focused and more confident in their analysis and reads, which can lead to even better results when they are playing well.

Overconfidence

Sometimes when you are running well you can get overconfident. When results are going your way, you may start to assume you are a better player than you actually are. Confidence is good in poker, but delusions of invincibility are not. You might try to play hands that you shouldn't because you believe you can "outplay your opponents after the flop." Alternatively, you might start paying less attention to the game assuming that the money will roll in regardless.[63] An online player might start surfing the net, or a live player might start watching the football game that's on TV in the background.

Also, the temptation to underestimate your bankroll requirements may arise. You start to think that recommended bankroll requirements don't apply to you because you are clearly such a good player. You might move up limits too early, not appreciating the pitfalls associated with such a decision.

Unrealistic expectations

Another problem a player on an upswing might face is assuming the good times will go on forever. We have already discussed that when you are on a downswing, you can often forget about the times when you were running well; the reverse is also true. You might start calculating how much you can make long-term based on unrealistic short-term figures. Even if you do remember to take into account the fact that you are running particularly well, you may still underestimate how badly things will eventually run. For example, a limit Hold'em player might have a train of thought that runs:

"In my last 3,000 hands, I have won six big bets per 100 hands. Even if I could just make four big bets per 100 hands over the long term, I could quit work and just play poker."

Of course, the above does not take into account that even four big bets per 100 hands is an unrealistic expectation for all but the very best

---

[63] Note that both of these are forms of tilt, as described in chapter 6.

players. In the worst-case scenario, a player thinking like this will quit his job and then find that he is unable to pay the bills when the inevitable downswing arrives.

Laziness

A player winning at a good rate will often lose the incentive to improve. He is happy with his win rate as it is, and doesn't see the need to spend time reading books, articles, and forums, or reviewing hands. Alternatively, he might be disciplined enough to go through the motions of study, but lacks real motivation, and as a result, his mind is elsewhere. He would rather think, for example, about what he is doing on Saturday night than about how to improve his flop play against loose-aggressive players.

Remember the attitude that is part of the Poker Mindset: Dedicate yourself to a continuous cycle of analysis and improvement. As soon as you stop trying to improve your game, it will decline. This may leave you in an uncomfortable position where you don't make enough money in your upswings to compensate for your downswings, turning you into a losing player.

Individually, these problems are infrequent, and fortunately are usually minor ones when you experience them. Despite this, it is still worth considering the potential psychological impact of upswings. Believe it or not, there are some players who play correctly when on a downswing, but their game goes to pieces when they are running well. Different stimuli affect different players in different ways.

When on an upswing, you should take reasonable precautions to ensure that you don't tilt and that you don't make any bad decisions. Continue to play good poker and don't get overconfident. Treat the upswing as what it is; merely a lucky run of cards. If you make any decisions based on your win rate, make sure it is your win rate measured across a large enough number of hands so that you can be confident the results are a reasonable representation of your long-term win rate and not just a short-term blip.

9.3. Tilt and Your Opponents' Mindset

One of the most profitable times at the poker table is when one or more of your opponents are on tilt. Some players even try to encourage tilt for just this reason. The more your opponents are on tilt, the more you can profit as a result. This section briefly discusses the merits and moral arguments of that type of strategy. Whether or not you specifically encourage players to tilt, it is important to get inside the mind of an opponent who is on tilt so that you can exploit the situation.

Encouraging tilt

So far, we have been looking at tilt as a negative thing. But since poker is a zero-sum game,[64] everything that is bad for one player must be good for another. Tilt can be a good thing when the person tilting is one of your opponents. In effect, we are trying to look at the Poker Mindset inside out. What attitudes of the Poker Mindset do our opponents lack and how can we take advantage of those weaknesses?

One or more of your opponents going on tilt is good news. What that player loses in expectation, the rest of the table collectively gains. If the tilt is slight, then each player at the table will individually gain very little (unless the game is short-handed). On the other hand, if the tilt is major, then each player could notice a significant increase in their expected win rate.

If an opponent going on tilt is good news, this poses two questions:

- Can we increase the likelihood of our opponents going on tilt?
- If so, should we?

---

[64] Actually, because of the rake, poker is a negative-sum game. However, the rake is a constant, and so, except in rare circumstances, poker is similar to a zero-sum game for illustration purposes.

The answer to the first question is yes. It is not easy and the results aren't always predictable, but there are things you can do to put an opponent on tilt. The answer to the second question is less clear, and one that we can't really provide completely. Some players would say that all is fair at the poker table; if you can do anything (within the rules of the game) to put your opponent on tilt, then you should do it. Others would argue that intentionally tilting your opponents is unsportsmanlike, and you should beat them without resorting to such tactics.

In reality, the "right" answer is probably somewhere in between these two extremes. Many players agree with the idea of trying to tilt an opponent in principle, but would shy away from any controversial methods that might make the game unpleasant for all involved or that loiter on the boundaries of gamesmanship and might even breach the rules.

For example, one strategy for putting a player on tilt might be to show a bluff. If a player sees he was bluffed, he might get angry for making a mistake or just because you showed him up in front of everyone at the table. Or you might call his raise with trash, hoping to get lucky and cause him to blow his top if you win the pot after showing a trash hand. Most poker players would consider these methods perfectly acceptable. At the other end of the scale, you might try to put a player on tilt by consistently berating him or even personally insulting him. Ethically, this tactic rests on shaky ground.

At the end of the day, each player must make his own decision about how far he is willing to go in order to win. We have repeatedly argued that you cannot afford to give up any edge at the poker table; however, we are prepared to concede a bit of ground when it comes to this contentious issue. The goal of poker is to win money, but it is important to do so in a way that allows you to feel happy with yourself afterwards. Poker is a game, but that shouldn't mean that all morals and courteous behavior are thrown out the window.[65]

---

[65] In fact, this type of behavior can sometimes lower your earnings if it drives bad players from the game.

Exploiting tilt

What you definitely *do* need to know is how to exploit an opponent who is on tilt, whether *you* put him on tilt, somebody else did, or (more likely) he managed to tilt by himself. To do this, you must get inside the mind of your opponent to understand his new motives so that you can make the correct adjustments. If you don't make these adjustments, you will not maximize the opportunity and could possibly even lose expectation.

The first thing you need to do is identify exactly *how* your opponent is tilting. As outlined in chapter 6, there are many different ways that someone can go on tilt, and if you make too many assumptions, you might get burned. For example, a player might start playing a lot of trash hands but still play well after the flop. He might play with the appropriate aggression pre-flop and on the flop, but then get extremely passive on the turn and river when the bets are bigger.

Once you have established how your opponent is tilting, it is simply a case of forgetting how he usually plays. You must treat him as if he were a completely different opponent, with the playing style you have observed. Once you identify his weaknesses, you will then need to make adjustments in your own play. For example, if he is playing too loose, then you will be playing better hands on average and so will be the favorite when you go heads up against him. On the other hand, you will have to be more careful about putting your opponent on a hand, because his range of hands will be wider.

One thing to remember about playing against a player on tilt is that his play is liable to change at any time. He may pull himself together and start playing his usual game, or (more likely) his play will deteriorate even further and he may tilt in new ways. Keep constant tabs on your opponent's play to get as much warning as possible when he changes gears.

Tilt is a part of the game. Remember that every player tilts at some point, and part of the game is to exploit your opponent's weaknesses.

Be careful not to fall into the trap of feeling sorry for your opponents and showing mercy; you can be sure they wouldn't show you any if the positions were reversed.

9.4. When Sub-optimal Is Optimal

Throughout this book we have stressed the importance of making the correct decision at every possible opportunity. The correct decision in this context has been the one that gives you the highest monetary expectation on the hand.[66]

But what about situations where you might want to sacrifice some expectation now in the hope of yielding a greater expectation in future hands? These situations do exist in poker and are worth discussing, particularly because players often have misconceptions about this area of the game.

So what kind of plays are we talking about here? We briefly mentioned one of them earlier in the chapter, which is making a sub-optimal play because there is a chance it might put your opponent on tilt. For example, you might call a raise with a weak hand that has potential, like 9-7 suited, against an opponent known for blowing his top. You might hit a big hand or draw on the flop, and if you don't, it is a relatively easy hand to get away from.

Probably the most well-known example of a sub-optimal play used for long-term benefit is what is called an advertising play. You make a play with a slightly lower expectation in the hope that the other players at the table make assumptions about your play based on that. Some examples are:

---

[66] We recognize that not everybody plays poker just to make money, and we will be dealing with this issue later in the chapter.

- Making a bluff that has a slightly negative expectation. You either win the pot or you get the benefit of your opponents calling and seeing your bluff, which can lead to a better chance of getting paid off later when you really do get a hand.
- Raising or calling a raise with a weak hand, hoping that your opponents will label you as a fish or a maniac, an image that you can then exploit.
- Playing extremely tightly for a period of time. Then, once your opponents think of you as ultra-tight, start raising more often, picking up lots of blinds because your opponents assume you are getting big hands.

How your opponents perceive your play is known as your *table image*. Manipulating your table image to your own ends can be profitable in certain circumstances, but this depends on a number of things. First, you have to be sure that your opponents are observing and reacting to your play. Second, you have to believe that you can convincingly sell the image.

Of course, there is no point trying to sell a table image to players who are not really paying attention to what you are doing anyway. If you are playing in a small stakes game against weak opposition, then you are probably better off not worrying about your table image at all. All that advertising plays will do is cost you short-term expectation. However, if you play at the higher limits or in big tournaments, then your table image becomes more important.

For example, let's assume that you are generally a tight player. Occasionally, you should get a little wild and raise pre-flop with a weak hand; otherwise, your observant opponents will back away and give you a lot of credit when you *do* raise with a big hand. You don't want opponents folding every time you have a premium hand. For example, in a limit game, you might raise on the button with 6-4 suited. No matter what happens, show this hand. You won't lose much in this one play, but the image that you sometimes play 64s will help you get paid off for quite some time.

Keeping the game friendly

Another reason you might make a sub-optimal play is to keep a game friendly. It isn't a common situation, but if you are playing with extremely weak players who are all having a good time and giving their money away, then you don't want to do anything that might upset this equilibrium. It is worth far more to you to keep those players happy and at the table than to win the absolute maximum from every hand.

For example, you have just made your nut flush on the river against a new player who you are pretty certain has two pair or a set. You think the best play is a check-raise because you are 80% certain he will bet if you check and then pay off the raise. However, you might want to consider just betting out. It will cost you a fraction of a big bet on average, and by betting you are saying, "I've made my hand and I'm letting you know so you don't lose too much money." Check-raising your opponent, on the other hand, could appear unfriendly and greedy.

Of course, we all know that there is nothing unfriendly at all about check-raising and that it is just part of the game. New players don't like being check-raised, though, and it might pay you in the long term to keep the game friendly. Encourage other players at the table to view you as a good but fair opponent. They may stick around longer, and next time they have some money to spare, they won't mind playing at your table.

With occasional exceptions, keeping the game friendly is rarely an important factor in online games. Online players rarely sit at the table for very long anyhow, so you are generally better off taking the short-term profit now while the weak player is still at the table.

Be careful when making sub-optimal plays

You may be able to come up with other scenarios in which it pays to make a sub-optimal play. However, what you must remember is that these plays are quite advanced and should be treated as such. You could have a very long and successful poker career without ever making a play for a reason other than expectation on that one hand.[67]

Some players will overuse these tricks and unfortunately use them for the wrong reasons. You should never use something like "table image" as an excuse to do something that you would like to do but know you shouldn't. Every play you make at the poker table must have a clearly defined purpose and be designed to maximize your expectation, if not in this hand, then at least in the long term.

9.5. Probability in Action

You are in bad shape as a poker player if you don't have at least a basic knowledge of probability. Probability is one of the fundamental building blocks upon which poker rests. It helps us to understand how the game works and to predict what will happen in a given situation. In fact, probabilities have a role in practically every decision you make at the poker table whether you realize it or not. Matthew discusses this topic in detail in his book *Texas Hold'em Odds and Probabilities: Limit, No-Limit, and Tournament Strategies*.

This section discusses some of the more-subtle ramifications of probability within poker. We will look at how poker players often misunderstand how probability really works, and as a result, how they cope badly with the random elements of the game.

---

[67] In fact, if you never made a decision other than for that reason, then your career is very likely to be long and successful.

Bad luck

Before we can even start discussing probability, there is one thing you *must* understand and accept.

You are not unlucky.

You are not lucky either. Neither is any other player particularly lucky or unlucky. If you believe you are lucky or unlucky, then you are putting yourself in a position where you might make bad decisions as a result of this viewpoint.

Convince yourself that you are neither lucky nor unlucky. Luck is a label that can only be applied in the past tense, never in the future. The odds of any random event occurring are precisely those dictated by the laws of probability. If you miss ten flush draws in a row, then the odds of hitting the next one are exactly the same as the odds of hitting the first one, or indeed any of the other nine. If you are considering how well you are running when you make a decision, then you are on tilt.

The majority of players have a tendency to think of themselves as unlucky. There are two reasons why, the most obvious being that most players lose. If you lose, then your alternatives are either to admit you don't have the skill to beat the game or to put your losses down to "bad luck." For most players, it is a major blow to the ego to admit the former, so it is easier to attribute their losses to bad luck. If these losses are consistent over the long term, you might decide you are simply an unlucky person rather than face the reality that you may not be as good a player as you thought.

The second reason is that bad luck tends to stick in your mind much more than good luck. People tend to think of luck as an unlikely event that has occurred in their favor, against the odds as it were. In reality, however, a likely event occurring in a person's favor can also be lucky as there was still the possibility of that event going the other way.

For example, let's say you are playing limit Hold'em and hold A♠ K♣. You raise pre-flop and are called by one player who has Q♥ J♠. The flop is A♥ J♦ 9♥. You bet and are called down all the way, scooping a modest pot when blanks fall on the turn and the river. Was this lucky on your part? Most people would say no, as you had the best hand on every street. You certainly wouldn't consider your opponent "unlucky" in this situation.

However, you were lucky in a sense. Pre-flop, you were only a 65% favorite to win the hand. On the flop, if both players go to showdown, you are still only a 76% (approximately 3:1) favorite. The fact you won the hand when your chance of winning was "only" 65% or 76% was lucky. You got a better result than you would expect on average. To add perspective, if this exact situation on the same flop occurred three times, then your chance of winning all of them is less than 50%.

When we play poker, we don't tend to notice when things go as planned. We don't notice when our flopped hand holds up, our aces *don't* get cracked, or our opponent's flush draw doesn't make it. Yet we suddenly sit up and take notice when we are "unlucky." We forget about all the times we were fortunate enough not to get outdrawn, focusing instead on this one hand, lamenting our bad luck.

Nobody is naturally unlucky. Over the course of your poker career, luck will not be a significant factor in your overall results. You will have individual hands, sessions, and even strings of sessions when your luck is bad, but this will all come close to evening out over the long term.

Action Point: It is often easier to rationalize luck if you are aware of the actual probabilities involved. See if you know the approximate answers to the following questions. The answers are revealed later in the chapter.

1. How often, on average, will you be dealt AA in Hold'em?
2. If you have a flush draw on the flop, what are the odds of making a flush by the river?
3. Approximately how often will A-K beat 44 if both players go to showdown?
4. If you have a pocket pair, how often will you flop a set?
5. What percentage of the time do unpaired starting hands flop a pair or better (not counting straights and flushes)? How often can you expect to flop exactly two pair?

Large sample sizes

Poker players often complain when they are struck by what seems like a very unlikely piece of bad luck. For example, maybe your opponent catches runner-runner quads on the turn and river to beat your flopped full house. Maybe you get two pairs of kings in a session, and both times one of your opponents has aces. Maybe you fail to flop a set 30 times in succession when you hold a pocket pair.

These are the kinds of stories that poker players everywhere love to tell. As mentioned in the previous section, a large proportion of players consider that they are unlucky, and these amazing streaks of bad luck seem to be evidence of that. Some will even quote to you the exact probability of such an event occurring, which is generally a tiny percentage.[68]

---

[68] In fact, the probabilities of the three events described above are approximately 0.1%, 0.19%, and 2.3% respectively.

However, if these players looked a stage further into the realm of probability, they would discover the truth about their incredibly "bad luck." While in any given hand or session, the chance of such an event happening is very small, it becomes much more likely when you are playing hundreds of hands per week, or hundreds of sessions per year.

Let's look at the pair of kings example. To make the calculation easier, we will assume that you get exactly two pairs of kings every session. If you play 156 sessions in a year (three per week), then the odds of this freak occurrence happening sometime in that year is now a significant 26%. Still not terribly likely, but now only a 3-1 shot rather than the 526-1 shot you had before.

It gets even worse. While the odds of *this particular* piece of bad luck happening in any given year are only 26%, what about all of the other possible things that could happen? There are three examples above, but in reality there are dozens of freak occurrences that individually might be unlikely, but collectively become quite likely to happen.

What if we assume there are just 50 possible pieces of freak bad luck (a completely arbitrary figure), and all of them had a 26% chance of occurring in any given year. You will experience, on average, 13 of these freak occurrences every year. Or, to put it another way, if you can tell each story for four weeks, you will perpetually have a really bad beat story to tell. Is it any wonder that casinos and poker forums are full of people telling "you won't believe what happened to me" stories?

If you play on the Internet, the "problem" is especially severe. Internet players can play literally thousands of hands per day if they play full time. Over the course of a year, a keen Internet player may play as many as half a million hands! In that time, pretty much anything that can happen, will happen. No wonder there are so many people who think that Internet poker sites are rigged.

Small probabilities

Poker players have a problem quantifying probabilities that are very small. In fact, this is not a problem confined to poker; it is a trait of people in general. For example, the national lottery in the UK generally has a jackpot of a couple of million pounds. The odds of winning this jackpot are around one in 14 million.[69]

A figure of 14,000,000:1 is difficult to quantify for most lottery players. While they recognize that their chances of winning are low, they don't realize quite how low. Fourteen million is such a large number that it is just mentally filed away under "a large number," and subsequently their chance of winning as "quite unlikely." It is doubtful that the sales of lottery tickets would be significantly different if those odds were one in 5 million, 20 million, 50 million, or even 500 million with the same payouts.

Probabilities don't need to be as low as one in 14 million to cause people problems. Poker players often have problems with numbers that appear far more manageable, either overestimating or underestimating their significance. For example, the odds of turning an unimproved pocket pair into a set on the turn are approximately one in 23. This doesn't stop some players holding pairs that are obviously beaten from paying to see the turn with considerably less than 23-1 pot odds.

It works the other way, too. A player chasing a marginal draw will often not stop to consider the (albeit small) possibility that he will make his hand and still lose. For example, most good players know that they have about a one in nine[70] chance of hitting a set on the flop when holding a pocket pair, but have no idea what the odds are of that set getting beaten. All they know is that "sets win most of the time."

The thing about poker is that every small probability is important. You need to look at the unlikely events as well as the likely events. If you are playing hundreds of hands of poker per week, then these little

---

[69] There are also smaller prizes. However, even taking these into account, the amount of the ticket proceeds paid out in prizes is only around 50%.

[70] The odds are actually 1 in 8.5, which we rounded in the text.

mistakes add up over time. A poker player needs an acute attention to detail to be successful. Make sure your decisions at the poker table are as good as they can possibly be.

Action Point: Here are the answers to the quiz earlier in the chapter.

1. Once every 221 hands
2. 35% (about 1 in 3)
3. 46% of the time (48% if suited)
4. 12% of the time (around 1 in 9)
5. Pair or better, 32% of the time (around 1 in 3). Exactly two pair, 2% of the time (around 1 in 49).

9.6. Internet and Live Play

One of our goals in writing this book was to provide advice that was relevant to all poker players, whether they play in traditional card rooms, or online in one of the many Internet poker rooms. To that end, we have put a lot of asides and footnotes into the main text to point out where something may apply only to live or only to Internet players, or where our recommendations differ depending on where you play.

In this section, we look at some of the differences between live and online play a bit more closely. Obviously, there are the basic differences that most players are aware of. When playing poker online, you:

- Have no face-to-face contact with your opponents.
- Can play more hands per hour.
- Can play at lower limits.
- Generally have a wider choice of games.
- Have less associated costs (tips, travel, etc.).
- Are reliant on your PC and Internet connection not failing.

Interesting as these are, in this book we are more concerned about the psychological impact of playing live or online. There are different pitfalls within each, and you must emphasize different elements of the Poker Mindset in order to be successful depending on whether you play live or online. The following is a guide to the differences between live and online play with regards to applying the Poker Mindset.

Slow pace of live games

Live games move a lot more slowly than online games. Shuffling, dealing, and counting chips all take time, and there is usually no time limit for players to make their move, unlike in online games. While actual speeds vary, online players probably play around 60-80 hands per hour,[71] while a live player will be lucky to play half that.

In live games, you will have a lot of time between hands with nothing much to do. Even while a hand is in progress, the action will proceed somewhat slowly. On the plus side, this means that a live player should have no excuse for not taking in everything. You have all the time in the world to analyze your opponent's decisions and make the best decisions yourself. After all, given that you are probably folding 75% of hands pre-flop, you will only be an active participant in one or two hands every ten minutes, so you should be able to focus all of your energy on those one or two hands.

However, the slow speed of live play also brings with it some problems. First, it is easy to get bored. Playing tight poker in a live game is somewhat akin to fishing. You will have long periods of inactivity interspersed with brief periods of excitement. If you are having a poor run of cards, it is easy to get bored and lose concentration and motivation. You may find yourself on formulaic tilt, becoming distracted by other things going on such as table chat or the TV in the background. This is especially true if you are an Internet player new to the live game and aren't used to the long waits.

---

[71] This assumes you are only playing one table at a time. Multi-table play will naturally increase this number dramatically.

Second, and more dangerously, you might start to relax your starting hand requirements in order to make things happen. A period of cold cards can go on for an incredibly long time when playing live. Sometimes you might go half an hour or more without playing a single hand, at which time it can be very tempting to relax your starting hand requirements a little just to get some action. Or when you do get a good starting hand, you might be reluctant to let it go if you don't hit the flop.

> Action Point: An excellent way to relieve the boredom in live games is to try to put your opponents on a hand when you are not involved in the hand yourself. This can be quite fun and is also excellent for improving your hand-reading skills.

How long is the long term?

Because online games move faster than live games, obviously the "long term" is reached a lot more quickly. Downswings (and indeed upswings) will last the same number of hands on average, all other things being equal. However, those hands are played at a quicker pace online and so will take less time to play through. For example, if a live player goes on a downswing of 5,000 hands, it will last for over 150 hours of play. By contrast, if an online player who plays two tables at once were to experience the same downswing, then it would only last approximately 30 hours.

This can potentially make downswings a lot easier to handle for the online player. Even for a casual player, 30 hours of play might only take a couple of weeks to get through. He won't experience that sinking feeling that the live player may sometimes get when he hasn't won any money for literally months. Individual sessions are more uniform, too. An online player is extremely unlikely to play a whole session without winning a hand, which is something that happens occasionally to live players.

However, there is a downside to all of this. While downswings tend to be over faster chronologically, they are also a lot more brutal. A downswing for an online player incorporates a lot of bad luck in a comparatively short period of time. A live limit player who is devastated by a 40-big-bet losing session should be thankful he is not an online player on the wrong end of a 100-big-bet beating, which is well within the realm of possibility. Additionally, if an online player tilts for, say, 30 minutes, that episode of tilt will lose him a lot more money because he will be playing more hands per hour when it happens. For an online player, therefore, it is even more important to stop playing at the first sign of tilt.

Distractions online

The hidden enemies of the online player are distractions. A live player has comparatively few to contend with. There may be a TV in the background, or his opponents may be very chatty, but on the whole he can concentrate on the cards because he doesn't have much else to do. An online player, on the other hand, has countless distractions including email, the Internet, games, TV, and family members. They must deal with these distractions while playing hands far more rapidly than a live player would.

Of course, the obvious solution is simply not to allow yourself to become distracted by these things, but in many cases this is easier said than done. If the TV is on in the background, sometimes you can't help but watch it. If you get a pop-up saying you have a new email, then it can be very tempting to read it. If your spouse or children talk to you, how can you simply ignore them? Unfortunately, the reality is that you will probably get distracted more playing online regardless of what you do. But there are some steps you can take to lessen the problem.

First, minimize the distractions that are available to you. Don't turn on the TV, or better yet, don't have a computer and TV in the same room. Don't have your email or the Internet open in the background, as you might be tempted to flick between them in between hands.

Tell your family that it is important that you concentrate fully when playing, so they shouldn't disturb you unless it is important. Create an environment where distractions are occasional rather than frequent.

Once you have created that environment, make sure that you are disciplined enough to take advantage of it. Don't "quickly check your email" or "quickly check the football score" while playing; otherwise, before you know it, you will be quickly checking them every five minutes. If you are bored enough that the temptation is too strong, then take a break. Come back to the game when you are ready to give it your total concentration.

Online accountability

Online poker is characterized by its ease of use and its abundance of choice. You can play any limit from $.01-$.02 to $200-$400 and even higher. You can play practically every type of game from Hold'em to Stud to Omaha and more. You can play in either full ring games or short-handed cash games, in multi-table tournaments or in single-table tournaments (usually referred to as SNGs or sit-n-go tournaments). You can move between these with the click of a button and even play multiple tables simultaneously. This is the beauty of online play, and also, for some players, its curse.

The problem is that because everything is so much easier and faster for an online player, making horrific, tilt-induced, bankroll-destroying decisions are far easier, too.

For example, let's say a live player is having a horrendous session playing $5-$10. He gets angry and frustrated and looks over at the $20-$40 table, thinking about how quickly he could get his money back if he wins a couple of pots there. He leaves the table and puts himself down on the list for the $20-$40 game. He then goes to the cashier and gets enough chips for the minimum buy-in, and waits for his seat. By now, he has had plenty of time to calm down and hopefully talk himself out of this foolish endeavor.

However, in the time it has taken the live player to get started, an online player would have opened the table, sat down, and quite likely lost a great deal of money. There are far fewer checks and balances preventing the online player from doing something. There is no waiting around for a seat, no friend at the casino seeing what you are doing and warning you against it, no strange looks from the regulars at the big game when you sit down, no opponents commenting that you appear to be angry. Even the cash doesn't seem as real to an online player. Handing $1,000 to the cashier for the buy-in at the $20-$40 game might be the point when you realize you are in over your head; an online player, however, just sees numbers on the screen.

This is another reason why emotional control and tilt avoidance are more important for online players. If they choose to do something stupid, they can do it literally at the click of a button. There is something else that you can do just as easily with the click of a button that would make far more sense: Switch off the PC.

Temptations of the casino

While online players can make expensive mistakes more quickly, live players in a casino have their own temptations to deal with. The most obvious of these are the little temptations sitting right outside the poker room: craps tables, roulette, slots, and, for many players, blackjack.[72] Everybody knows that these games are losing propositions, but they can be very tempting if you are stuck and want a quick way to get back to even.

That's not to say that it is definitively wrong to play games other than poker. If you play responsibly, games in which the casino has an edge are just another way of paying for entertainment, like spending money on going to a movie or a ballgame. Just take heed of two warnings:

---

[72] We say "many players" for blackjack because, under certain circumstances, it is possible to play blackjack with positive expectation. However, most players don't understand the game well enough to profit from it.

1. Never use these games in an attempt to "get back to even." In the long term, you will lose money at these games, so the most likely scenario is that you will just make a bad situation worse.

2. Don't gamble at stakes that will seriously eat into your poker winnings. There is no point in playing poker for three hours with an expected earn rate of $20 per hour and then playing roulette for an hour with $20 bets on your way out. If you really must play these games, play at stakes as small as you can bear, and try not to do it every time you play poker. If you get into the habit of gambling in games you can't beat, it can end up being a huge leak.

There are other less-obvious things that tempt you in a casino, which can lead to additional losses. The big hidden enemy of many players is alcohol. Why do many casinos give you free alcohol when you are playing? It's not because they are especially generous, but because they know you are more likely to play longer if you are not only getting something "for free" but if you're also drunk.

Drinking alcohol is a bad idea when playing for meaningful stakes. If you can't resist getting a drink when the cocktail waitress comes around (it will only cost you a $1 tip, after all), then get something non-alcoholic. It is impossible to know how much your play is adversely affected by alcohol, which varies from player to player, so why take the chance?

> Action Point: It can be fun to drink while playing poker and you can! If you want to drink, play at low limits where the money you lose is not meaningful to you. If it is something you enjoy, then play one session per week in a low limit or home game where you can relax, unwind, and have fun with a few drinks without losing significant money.

Remember that when playing poker in a casino, it is often more difficult to walk away when you know you should. You may have had a long journey to get there and planned a good five-hour session at the tables. It is difficult after an hour to quit and go home for a "small" reason, such as playing badly or not finding a good game. You might be tempted to carry on playing, or you might make the right decision and quit but then spend all of your money somewhere else, like the bar, the buffet, or the craps table.

Casinos are designed to make you spend money, so unless you are playing poker with an edge, you really want to spend as little time in them as possible.

9.7. Professional Poker

Anyone who has ever won money at poker, even only in the short term, has probably fantasized about what it would be like to play poker for a living. To forgo "real work" and just sit in a casino (or at a PC) all day playing a game you love can seem like an ideal way to make a living. This fantasy is propagated by the fact that there are a lot of professional poker players, and the advent of Internet poker has made it more viable to play for a living. A lot of winning players wonder if they could go pro.

If you wonder whether you have what it takes to make it as a professional poker player, or you are already planning to take the plunge, then you need to read this section. If you think it doesn't apply to you (which should be most of you), then feel free to either skip it or read it as a matter of interest.

The important thing to realize is that every poker player is different. For one player, it might make sense to go pro, while for another of a similar playing standard, it might be a bad move. The decision is one that must be made according to your exact strengths, weaknesses, and personal circumstances. If anybody approached us and asked if they should become a professional poker player, then we would probably err on the side of caution and say no. This is the safe answer, because most players (even most winning players) do not have what it takes to be successful at professional poker. You will never go far wrong by sticking to your day job and keeping poker as a lucrative hobby.

But of course there are people who have turned pro and done very well for themselves. If you think you can be one of those people, then you must make sure you have every angle covered. In this section, we pose a number of questions that you must have satisfactory answers to before you can make that decision.

1. Are you good enough?

Of course, the most obvious question is whether or not you are a good enough player to turn pro. Remember, the long term in poker is very long indeed, and having good results for a couple of months is no basis on which to make a decision like this. To even think about turning pro, you will need to be a proven winner over a large number of hands (at least 50,000, preferably a lot more) at the limit you intend to play.

Unfortunately, it is very difficult to know how good you really are from a statistical perspective. For example, after 1,000 hours of play, it is still possible that you are a losing player, even though you are showing good results. Not every player, especially live players, will want to play enough hands to statistically know they are beating the game. The answer needs to come from within. Do you really understand why you are winning? Do you recognize all of the mistakes your opponents are making? In the end, you will probably need to gamble a little before taking the big step, but try to make it a small gamble rather than a big one.

2. Can you make enough money?

If you are contemplating a change in career, you will naturally want to know how much you can expect to earn. Fortunately, if you know your long-term earn rate and can do some simple math, then your expected "take-home pay" is easy to calculate. Simply multiply your hourly earn rate by the number of hours you intend to work. You have to be realistic about your working hours. In the long term, you won't want to work 7 days a week, 10 hours a day, for the rest of your life.

Whether this is enough money is, of course, entirely subjective and will depend on your expectations and what you could earn elsewhere. One of the main reasons why professional poker might not be a great career choice for most people is that if you are sharp enough to earn good money playing poker, then you are probably clever enough to earn good money in other fields without the uncertainly that professional poker entails. Make sure that you can earn enough money to support your lifestyle and are not taking a big pay cut because you are seduced by the idea of playing poker instead of working a real job.

Also, take into account that there are lots of hidden expenses for a professional poker player. You will receive no paid holidays and no sick pay. If you take a vacation or can't work one day because you are ill, then this comes straight out of your paycheck. You also won't receive benefits such as health insurance or life insurance. If you want these things (health insurance is almost a must for US residents), then you will need to pay for them yourself.

3. Do you have a sufficient bankroll?

We spent a lot of time in chapter 7 discussing the importance of bankroll management. Yet if you are planning on playing professionally, then the recommendations in chapter 7 are woefully inadequate. A professional player needs a much larger bankroll than a casual player for a number of reasons:

1. Their bankroll is their livelihood. If they lose their bankroll, then they no longer have a means to make money.
2. They will be withdrawing a portion of their bankroll each month, making it far more likely that they will go broke.
3. A larger bankroll lessens the pressure to make money in any given month.

A good starting point would be to double the recommended bankroll requirements in chapter 7. If you plan on going pro, make sure you have the required bankroll before you start. There is no such thing as a bankroll that is too big.

4. Do you have a plan?

If you plan on going pro, you should have a solid plan of what you intend to do on a day-to-day basis and also in the longer term. How many days per week (and which ones) will you play? How many hands (or hours) per day? Which hours will you play? Which game will you play and at what limit? Will you play limit, no-limit, tournaments, or a mixture? How many vacation days will you take per year? When will you set aside time to study the game?

You have a far better chance of succeeding as a professional if you work all of this out before you start rather than make it up as you go along. In fact, it would be a good idea to try out your plan for a week to iron out any flaws, before quitting your day job. Unforeseen problems may crop up, such as the games not being very good at the times you propose to play or your shifts being shorter than you planned

5. Are you disciplined enough?

We are not talking so much about discipline at the table (although this is obviously of paramount importance for any player), but rather about the discipline to put in enough hours and play enough hands. As a professional poker player, you are your own boss, which brings freedom but also responsibility. If you are the kind of person who has trouble motivating himself or is prone to taking "sick days," then professional poker is probably not the career for you.

If you are woken by your alarm clock and want a couple of extra hours' sleep, then you can have them. If you are bored halfway through your session and want to go home, then you can; there is nobody to stop you. But all of this will catch up to you when, at the end of the month, you haven't played enough hours and have trouble paying the bills. The freedom you get from playing professionally can be as much of a curse as a blessing if you are undisciplined.

6. How will you cope emotionally in a bad month?

If you have read the rest of this book (especially chapter 5), then this topic should be fresh in your mind. All players experience downswings from time to time, professional players included. What matters is how you react when you are on a downswing. Do you continue to play your best game in spite of your bad luck, or do you lose confidence, go on tilt, and become obsessed with your losses? If you have problems in this area (and still have problems even after reading this book), then professional poker is almost certainly not for you.

The problem is that once you play professionally, poker is no longer a game as such; it is your livelihood. Casual players might have problems coping with downswings, but at the end of the session, they can leave poker behind and get on with the rest of their life. For a professional player, the two are intertwined. Quality of life is directly linked to success at the poker table to the extent that if a pro doesn't win any money for long enough, he won't be able to afford even the bare essentials. While this should never happen to a properly bankrolled winning player, it will certainly prey on his mind when things are going badly. Anger, depression, and frustration are familiar foes for a player on a downswing. A professional player might have to deal with all of these, plus fear and eventually panic.

7. How will you cope financially in a bad month?

This is the more practical and, in truth, simpler side of coping with a downswing. The hard part is developing the Poker Mindset necessary to cope with downswings. The easy part is practicing prudent financial planning so that if you do hit a bump in the road, your life won't start to unravel. Ideally, you would like to be in a situation where you can make no money at all for a few months, yet still be able to pay all the bills and live the exact same lifestyle as you do in the good months.

How you do this is up to you. The most obvious way is to have a number of months' worth of living expenses saved up before you start, maybe even a year's worth to be on the safe side. This will mean you can play your game without having any pressure to win for a long time. Alternatively, maybe you have an income from a second job or an investment that can provide you with extra cash when needed. Maybe you have a wife, husband, or partner who earns enough to support the both of you when you have a tough month. How you plan on coping through the bad months is entirely up to you; the important thing is that you know how. As a professional, you will have bad months, and it is important to know beforehand how you will deal with them.

8. What will your friends and family think?

Although poker is now very much in the mainstream, there are still a lot of people who disapprove of it for various reasons. Don't expect your parents, partner, or friends to be thrilled when you reveal you want to quit your job to become a professional gambler. Some will have religious or moral objections, while others will just be worried that you are giving up a guaranteed income for something more risky. If you plan on going pro, make sure you think about everyone that this decision will affect and discuss it with them.

Of course, you shouldn't necessarily allow one disapproving person to completely derail your well-thought-out plans. The important thing is to be open about what you are doing and try to ease specific concerns that person might have. Many, if not most, will be caused by misconceptions people have about poker. However, if someone who is directly affected by your decision (e.g., your spouse) seriously objects to it, then you may have to can the plan for the time being. By doing it against their wishes, you are really putting a lot of pressure on yourself to get good results and fast.

9. Will you get bored with the game?

While playing poker all day, every day, seems like a great career, it is unrealistic to think that the game will be as fun as a full-time job as it is as a hobby. Do anything for long enough, and it eventually loses its appeal; poker is no exception. From experience, we can tell you that when you are a professional poker player, your enjoyment and enthusiasm for the game will diminish. It won't disappear completely (at least, hopefully not), but there will be times that playing will seem more like a chore than something you actually want to do.

There is not a lot you can do about this, but two things are important. First, you should go in with your eyes open. Don't assume that you will be living a life of leisure and enjoying every minute of your day, because you won't. Second, think about how much you enjoy the game at present. Do you genuinely enjoy the game or do you just enjoy winning money? If it's the latter, then you will probably get very bored very quickly playing professionally. Making money is not so fun when you have to make money to live. It will become another job, and a stressful, sometimes tedious one at that. The game you love could now turn into just another job.

10. Is this what you want to do with your life?

Once the initial excitement has worn off, you might realize that being a professional poker player isn't really what you want to do with your life. As a career, it certainly has its positive side, but taking a more long-term view, you may find it less than fulfilling. Think about the future. Is this what you want to be doing five or ten years from now? Is sitting in front of a computer 40 hours a week for ten years really that glamorous?

Some players may also feel unfulfilled when they realize that they are simply making a living by taking other people's money. After a while, you might question this from an ethical standpoint or because it gives you no job satisfaction. Most people can come home from work feeling like they at least have achieved something or made a small difference in somebody's life. A poker player will have just redistributed wealth slightly, hopefully in his favor.

Whether this will ever be an issue for you naturally depends on what kind of person you are. Some professional poker players play for years without ever worrying about these things. Likewise, some players might wake up one morning questioning what they are giving back to the world. Think hard about whether in ten years' time you will be satisfied with a poker career, or whether you would have preferred to spend that time doing something more rewarding.

There are solutions to this problem. You could use part of the money you earn to help others. Get involved in charities and donate to special causes. Coordinate special charity poker tournaments in your area. You might even want to donate a specific percentage of your earnings to your favorite charity. That way, while your poker career won't make a direct contribution to society, it can make a big difference indirectly and may help you to make peace with the career you have chosen.

11. What is your backup plan?

This is the most important question of all. In fact, if you have a really good answer to this question, you can get away with having sub-standard answers for some of the others. Quite simply, you need to know what you will do if professional poker doesn't work out for you. What if you don't make as much money as you thought? What if you don't enjoy it? What if you can't handle the pressure of an uncertain income? What if poker loses popularity and the games dry up?

That is not to say that any of the above will happen for sure, but it is important to plan what you will do in that eventuality. Maybe you can keep some doors open in your current career so you can go back in where you left off. Or maybe you can study a new career while you are playing, which you can dive straight into if poker doesn't work out. Just make sure there is something there to fall back on so that professional poker isn't your only shot at success. Naturally, this means that if you are still in college, make sure you graduate before you dedicate too much time to poker. The games will still be there when you've finished, and your college degree will be something good to fall back on.

Conclusion

There is a lot to think about for anyone aspiring to become a professional poker player. It is not an easy alternative to a real job, nor is it necessarily glamorous, exciting, or going to make you rich. However, it can be a rewarding career if you enjoy the game enough and can handle the uncertainty that it brings. If you are seriously considering turning pro, make sure you can answer all of the questions above satisfactorily and talk to anyone that the decision might affect. It may also be worth talking over your idea with an existing poker pro, in case he brings up an issue you haven't thought of.

If you do decide to give it a go, we wish you the best of luck.

9.8. Non-Profit Motives

So far in this book, we have assumed that your only goal when playing poker is to make money. There are two reasons for this:

1. It's easier. It would have been impossible to teach the correct mindset and attitude for players with every single motive for playing.
2. If you are reading a book about poker, it is probably because you want to be more successful. You don't need a book to tell you, for example, how to have fun.

However, we recognize that some of you may be playing for reasons other than making money. In fact, because most players are long-term losers at poker, it stands to reason that most players play for reasons other than making money. Saying that poker should be played purely for money is almost too simplistic. Even winning players will normally have other motives as well. Here are some examples of other reasons why people play poker:

Recreation – Some people just enjoy playing the game of poker. They play because it is something fun to do in their spare time.

Gambling – Gamblers see poker as just another game in which they can try to get lucky.

Socializing – To some players, poker is about the people they meet. They will play in the same casino each week to see friends and either socialize with the same group of players or meet new ones. The game is more or less something that goes on in the background.

The challenge – Some players play poker for the mental challenge in the same way that people play other games or do crosswords to stimulate their minds.

These are the most common reasons people give for playing poker, but of course, there are others. You will find scores of people in casinos who claim to "play for the money" but are lifetime habitual losers, and these are frustrated and unhappy players. There is nothing wrong with being a recreational player if that's what you want to be, but a recreational player who thinks he is playing for the money will live a tortured existence.

If you are someone who plays for reasons other than money, then you must be honest with yourself.

Action Point: Make an honest assessment of why you play poker, listing all the reasons in order of how important they are to you. Return to this list every so often and make changes where necessary. This will keep you focused on why you play and allow you to make the best decisions accordingly.

The problem is that if you have motives other than making money, then you will have conflicts of interest. In a way, playing for money is quite a simple way to play poker. All you have to worry about is what play will yield the highest expectation in the long term. If you have other motives, then decisions become more difficult:

You know the call has negative expectation, but you really want to see what he has.

You know you shouldn't play this hand, but you are in the mood to gamble.

You know you should be concentrating on the game, but you are having a discussion with your buddy Jake about his new car.

You know you should play in a softer game, but you want to challenge yourself against the best players in the room.

If any of the above sound familiar, then it is time to make a decision. Do you want to play to win or do you want to pander to your other desires? There is no real middle ground: if you want to be a winning player, you have very little room to maneuver. You can't be, for example, a winning player who likes to gamble with sub-par hands, because you just don't have a big enough edge to do that and still make money.

If you would rather remain a recreational player, a gambler, or whatever else, then that is okay. It is the easier path, and provided you play with money you can comfortably afford to lose, you will enjoy your time at the tables. Remember, you can still try to play good poker and improve your game; you will just be doing it on your own terms. Hopefully, the information in this book will still help you approach the game in the right way and manage your more destructive emotions.

Alternatively, if you want to follow the path of the winning player, then you have to devote yourself to it. Study hard and play the way you know you should. It might not be as fun as the way you want to play, but it is the only way you will become a consistent winner. The reward is that you have the opportunity to make money out of something you enjoy. Poker is a fun game, but it's even more fun when you win! Just because you are a winning player doesn't mean you can't enjoy the game. It just means that you have to put winning money first when making decisions.

Whatever your decision, it doesn't have to be final. Many casual recreational players have made the step up to becoming winning players, while other former winning players no longer have the skills to win and just play recreationally.

Just be honest with yourself and make the decision that is right for you.

9.9. Chapter Review

❏ 9.1. When to Quit
- From a poker point of view, there are only two reasons why you ever need to end your session:
  1. You are no longer playing your best (i.e., you are on tilt).
  2. You are unable to beat the game (or find another within your bankroll that you can).
- There is absolutely no point in quitting because you are winning, and very little point in quitting purely because you are behind.
- Don't look at each session as a fresh start; instead, look at each hand as a fresh start, not to be influenced by any hands that have come before it.
- If you are unable to reach the stage where you accept losses or are indifferent to them, then setting stop-loss limits is a good idea.

❏ 9.2. What about Upswings?
- There are still dangers associated with being on an upswing; they are just less severe than those you face when on a downswing:
  - Overconfidence
  - Unrealistic expectations
  - Laziness

❏ 9.3. Tilt and Your Opponents' Mindset
- Tilt can be a good thing when the person tilting is one of your opponents.
- Whether or not you should encourage tilt and how far you might go to achieve your aim is up to each individual to decide.
- At the end of the day, poker is a game, but that shouldn't mean that all morals and courteous behavior are thrown out the window.

- It is important to know how to exploit an opponent who is on tilt, whether *you* put him on tilt, somebody else did, or (more likely) he managed to tilt by himself:
  - The first thing you need to do is identify exactly *how* your opponent is tilting.
  - Once you have established how your opponent is tilting, it is simply a case of forgetting how he usually plays. You must treat him as if he were a completely different opponent, with the playing style you have observed.

❏ 9.4. When Sub-optimal Is Optimal

- There are some situations where you might want to sacrifice some expectation now in the hope of yielding a greater expectation in future hands.
- Manipulating your table image to your own ends can be profitable in certain circumstances.
- One reason to make a sub-optimal play is to keep a game friendly when playing with extremely weak players.
- Be careful not to overuse these types of plays to justify in your mind plays which have a negative expectation.

❏ 9.5. Probability in Action

- Probability has a role in practically every decision you make at the poker table.
- The majority of players have a tendency to think of themselves as unlucky because most players lose and bad luck tends to stick in your mind much more than good luck.
- When we play poker, we don't tend to notice when things go as planned.
- Events that might seem like incredibly bad luck should actually be expected when you consider the thousands of possible events which are unlikely and the thousands of hands you are playing.

❑ **9.6. Internet and Live Play**

* The relative slow play of live play gives some players unique challenges, especially for the Internet player more accustomed to quicker play.

* Downswings can be a lot easier to handle for the online player since they should be relatively shorter in nominal terms given the speed of online play.

* On the downside, a downswing for an online player incorporates a lot of bad luck in a comparatively short period of time.

* The hidden enemies of the online player are distractions.

* One problem for the online player is the ease in which you can enter new games or new limits. This makes it easier to make horrific, tilt-induced, bankroll-destroying decisions.

* Casinos are designed to make you spend money, so unless you are playing poker with an edge, you really want to spend as little time in them as possible.

❑ **9.7. Professional Poker**

* There are some key questions a player should ask himself before turning pro:
  1. Are you good enough?
  2. Can you make enough money?
  3. Do you have a sufficient bankroll?
  4. Do you have a plan?
  5. Are you disciplined enough?
  6. How will you cope emotionally in a bad month?
  7. How will you cope financially in a bad month?
  8. What will your friends and family think?
  9. Will you get bored with the game?
  10. Is this what you want to do with your life?
  11. What is your backup plan?

❑ 9.8. Non-Profit Motives

- The main goal in poker is to make money, but there are other reasons why people play poker:
  - Recreation
  - Gambling
  - Socializing
  - The challenge
- If you are someone who plays for reasons other than money, then you must be honest with yourself.
- The problem is that if you have motives other than making money, then you will have conflicts of interest which get in the way of always making the decision which will yield the highest expectation in the long term.

Chapter 10

Poker and Life

"It is always good to remember that there is another world out there beyond the poker-room windows." – Larry W. Phillips
(from *Zen and the Art of Poker*)

10.1. The Missing Component of the Poker Mindset

The Poker Mindset focuses on the best-possible attitudes to take to the poker table for the purpose of maximizing your winnings. However, looking at the broader picture, there is actually a key component that is missing. This component is just as important as all the others, if not more so, but also acts as a counterpoint to them. This component may not (directly) maximize your winnings, but it will maximize the positive impact that poker has on your *life.*

The missing component is this: *Remember, poker is just a game.*

In many ways, this might be the most important attitude you can take to the table. There are much more important things in life than poker or making money, and you should not lose that perspective. The first seven attitudes of the Poker Mindset focused on maximizing your winnings at the poker table. Now with this missing component you can achieve true success.

At its roots, poker is a game that should be fun to play. If you no longer enjoy playing or are letting poker affect other areas of your life, then you need to reassess your attitude toward the game.

What you really want to maximize in poker is not the money you win, but the positive impact it has on your life as a whole. Of course, winning money is one way that poker can have a positive influence on your life, which is why it is a worthy goal. However, poker might also have a number of negative effects on your life.

- Maybe you spend too much time at the table and neglect your friends and family.
- Maybe you no longer enjoy the game, and it is becoming more like work than a hobby.
- Maybe the stress of playing poker is making you irritable, restless, or depressed when you are away from the table.
- Maybe the time you spend playing poker has forced you to give up other hobbies and interests you used to enjoy.

By mastering the first seven attitudes of the Poker Mindset, you might do an excellent job of making good poker decisions to win a lot of money at the table. But even while you are winning, poker may have turned into something that is more of a negative influence on your life than a positive one. Ironically, the bad players or "fish" that you look down on might actually do better from poker than you do. Although they lose money, they might get a lot of pleasure from the more-intangible things that playing poker offers, such as the thrill of gambling, the social interaction, the mental challenge, and the actual "fun" element of the game.

In the previous chapter, we discussed your motives for playing. Success is about fulfilling your objectives at the poker table, not necessarily winning the most money. Maybe you think that your only objective at the poker table *is* to win money. If that is the only reason you play, then poker is basically a job for you. In that case, make sure it is a job you are happy doing. Does the money you earn fully compensate for the work you put into the game both at the table and away from it? If not, then it is a rotten job! You might as well just put in more overtime at your day job, or find another part-time job to earn money.

If you are a professional poker player, you obviously need to take the game seriously. After all, it is your livelihood, and you have to support yourself and your family if you have one. However, if you are not having fun while "working" at the tables, then something has gone wrong. Do you remember why you became a professional poker player in the first place? Most pros were probably unhappy with their jobs and decided that poker would be a fun and fulfilling way to make a living. If you no longer enjoy poker, maybe you should rethink your career choice.

The emotional paradox of poker

The Poker Mindset talks about removing all emotion from decisions. By removing your emotions, you avoid going on tilt to help maximize your expectation at the table. The problem is that emotions are one of the things that make poker fun. It should be exciting when a crucial card is coming on the river. You should be happy when you win a big pot and disappointed when you lose.   When you completely remove emotions from the game, you end up with a bland game that is more like an exercise in intermediate mathematics than the thrilling, adrenaline-pumping roller coaster that it can be. Whether or not this is a bad thing depends on your point of view, but it certainly removes an element of the game that some people enjoy.

In chapter 4 we talked about the stages of dealing with a lost pot, in ascending order of desirability: Anger, Frustration, Acceptance, and Indifference. At the time, we considered indifference to be the best stage to reach, the stage where your short-term results do not matter at all and you are only concerned with making the correct decisions and learning from your mistakes. But you could argue that indifference is a stage too far. Do you *want* to be completely indifferent to your results, or would you like to keep that edge of emotion in the game? Would you like to play poker like a robot, or do you want the excitement of winning a pot and the disappointment of losing one?

There is no correct answer to this question, but therein lies what we call the emotional paradox of poker. You enjoy playing poker because

258 The Poker Mindset: Essential Attitudes for Poker Success

it is an exciting game. It is even more fun when you win money, so you try to adopt a mindset that will give you the best chance of making money. However, go too far with this mindset, and you could lose the very thing that you enjoyed about the game in the first place. We are not saying it is wrong to be indifferent about your results. From a poker results standpoint, indifference is an excellent place to be. Just make sure that you don't become so detached from the game that poker is no longer an enjoyable activity for you.

What we would really like to do is add a caveat to a part of the Poker Mindset: While you need to "Remove All Emotion from Decisions," that doesn't mean you should necessarily remove all emotions from your game full stop. Imagine winning a major poker tournament and feeling indifferent because you consider the win just an upbeat in your long-term results of ups and downs. Wouldn't it be more fun to be the guy who yells and gets emotional, hugging the crowd and showering himself with money? It is okay to get excited when you win a pot, and it is okay to be disappointed when you lose one — just make sure that your emotions do not interfere with your decision-making.

Remember, poker is just a game.

10.2. Life Beyond the Poker Table

Poker appeals to such a broad spectrum of people because it works on so many levels. For some of us, it is and will always remain a hobby. Poker is a way to meet people and to relax by doing something fun once or twice a week. For others, it is something far more significant — an interest that we are willing to devote a lot of time and energy to, in order to become better and more successful players.

It is likely that a fair proportion of people reading this book are in the latter group, purely because these are the players more likely to read poker books. There is nothing at all wrong with being a dedicated player. In fact, if you want to be successful at poker, it is effectively a requirement that you devote a lot of time to the game. It can take a great deal of learning and experience before you can beat even the middle limits consistently.

Although you may spend a lot of time at the table, the important thing is not to do so at the expense of the rest of your life. It is possible to get so immersed in poker that you forget the reason you started playing in the first place, which is usually because it was fun or because you wanted to try to make some extra cash. For the rest of this chapter, we'll look at how to successfully integrate poker with the rest of your life. As discussed in the previous section, true success at the poker table is measured by the influence it has on the rest of your life. You can be a big winner at the tables but still be all the worse for playing poker.

Some players go too far and play the game to the extent that it is no longer fun, or that the money they make is effectively worthless because they never spend it on anything that is *real*. This is one reason why, in chapter 7, we advised against *never* withdrawing any of your winnings (unless you still play at very low limits). It is an indication that to some extent you are missing the whole point of the game, even though, strictly speaking, it might be the best move for your poker career.

Remember there is more to life than poker. You don't need to be playing, studying, or thinking about the game every free hour you have in order to be successful. You can be a feared player at the felt and still have time for other important areas of your life such as family, friends, and your career. For a truly balanced life, you should also have time for other hobbies, whether it is golf, music, sports, travel, or anything else that interests you.

There are three reasons for this. First, it is simply healthier to have a life away from the poker table. You only get one shot at life, so do you really want to spend it all inside casinos or glued to your PC screen when there is a whole world out there? Younger players especially should try to diversify their interests, lest when they are older, they regret spending the best years of their lives just playing poker.

Second, poker as we know it might not last forever. It would be nice to think that it will remain immensely popular and claim its rightful place among other sports that have stood the test of time. However, poker's current popularity may not last forever. It might turn out to be no more than a fad (albeit a particularly prolific one), destined to decline in popularity as the weak players start to lose interest in the game. At this point, the games might get a lot tougher as the better players will be the ones who stick around. There is also the economic factor. The worldwide economy, especially in the United States, has given many players disposable income with which to risk and learn the game. Right now, we don't know the impact an economic recession will have on the game as a whole. And of course, there is the uncertain legal status of poker, particularly online poker in the United States, which may not have a certain resolution for many, many years.

Whether poker becomes a victim of the law or simply loses popularity, you will probably want other interests to fall back on. It is impossible to tell whether or not poker will still be popular in ten years' time, but if it isn't, you might regret having spent a large portion of your life on something that is of no use to you anymore. Poker is a great hobby to have; just make sure that you pursue other things that you enjoy, too.

The third reason to maintain a life outside poker is that you may suffer burnout. If you live and breathe poker all day, every day, there may come a time when it is no longer fun. Many keen players give up poker because the game loses its appeal after they play it so much. It starts to feel more like work and less like a hobby. If you have other hobbies and priorities in life, you are far less likely to experience this burnout.

If you play a lot of poker, it can be difficult to know where the game ends and the rest of your life begins. You need to draw boundaries to successfully integrate poker with the rest of your life, and vice versa. Allowing poker to take over your life can cause you much unhappiness in the long term. On the flip side, allowing the rest of your life to interfere with your game at the poker table can have much the same result.

10.3. Bankroll Separation

In chapter 7, we spent some time talking about the importance of bankroll management. The very idea of bankroll management is alien to some players because they don't make a clear distinction between their poker bankroll and their day-to-day finances in the first place. When they play poker, they withdraw money from the ATM or use whatever is in their pocket, but they never really have a separate bankroll used solely for poker.[73]

Some players do manage to keep a separate poker bankroll, but do not have the discipline to keep it completely independent from their other finances. If they want to buy something and don't have the cash available, they take money out of their poker bankroll. If their poker bankroll runs low, they pad it with money from their own pocket. This is a disorganized way of managing your finances that is a breeding ground for bad habits, delusion, and stress.

In fact, there are five distinct reasons that you should keep your poker bankroll completely separate from the rest of your day-to-day finances:

1. It enables good bankroll management.

If you have a clearly defined poker bankroll, it is much easier to exercise good bankroll management. You know exactly how much money you have available, so can make an informed calculation about what limit you can afford to play at, per the advice given in chapter 7.

If your bankroll is not clearly defined, then it is much harder to practice proper bankroll management. You might know exactly how much money you need for a given limit, but have no idea if you actually have that amount or not. You might have the money in your account

---

[73] This mainly applies to live players. Internet players always have a certain degree of separation because they have a set amount of money in their online poker account. Very few Internet players cash out and re-deposit every time they play.

now, but is it likely to be raided at any time to buy food, clothes, or pay the bills? Or maybe you don't have that money available now, but you will in a week when you get paid. The whole concept of bankroll management becomes extremely woolly when you don't have a set bankroll. You may convince yourself that you have the money to play at a particular limit when you actually don't.

2. You know how much you're winning or losing.

If you keep your bankroll separate from your day-to-day income and expenses, then it is easy to see how much you are winning or losing over a given period of time. If your bankroll is $500 but a month later it is $300, then you will know that you have lost $200.

If you have no clearly defined bankroll, however, gauging the loss will be far more difficult. If that $200 loss was over a month, then it is unlikely you suffered a steady stream of losses over that period. It is more likely to have been a hotchpotch of winning and losing sessions, sometimes clumped together in upswings and downswings, sometimes alternating or in pairs. In fact, with no clear poker bankroll, it might be difficult to tell whether you have won or lost over the course of the month, let alone by how much.

Of course, you can also track your wins and losses by keeping good records. The problem is that some players simply aren't very good at recording their results on a consistent basis. Also, it is easy to forget to record a session or to "cheat" and say that a particular session doesn't count since you were tired or drinking or whatever other reason you can come up with. Even if you do keep good records, a separate bankroll is helpful in reconciling the two to ensure that your records are accurate.

Obviously, it is very difficult to make any objective assessment of your poker game when you don't know how much you are winning or losing. Worst of all, long-term losing players will tend to believe they are actually winning. This sounds like a strange assumption to make, but it really isn't. Most poker players suffer from delusion to some extent, tending to overestimate their ability relative to others. Because poker literature is resolute in its assertion that the best players *will* make money in the long term, most players think they should be winning money. In the absence of any hard figures, they will in fact assume that they *are* winning money. People are good at seeing things they want to see and ignoring things they don't. A hazy memory of a month of up-and-down results will tend to aggregate to a win for a disorganized player who is deluded about his skill.

3. It lessens the pressure to win.

If your poker bankroll and your real-life finances are intertwined, then the inevitable result is that your poker fortunes and your overall financial security also become intertwined. Losing a lot of money at poker will prove to be a drain on your finances. If you have good results at the tables, you will be able to spend more money on other things.

This can cause you plenty of problems. Even if you only gamble with what you can afford to lose — and so avoid the problem of a downswing causing you serious financial problems — you're still under a lot of pressure to get good results at the table. Every winning session represents a night out, a new outfit, or new furniture. It will be much harder to remove yourself from the short term and make the best decisions for long-term profitability.

If you have a bankroll that stands on its own, you can distance yourself more easily from your short-term results. A bad session won't matter; it won't affect your life away from the table in any way. This takes the pressure off you and allows you to concentrate on making the best decisions. The game will be more enjoyable rather than seem like a job.

4. It allows you to play with large sums of money.

An interesting side effect of having an independent poker bankroll is that you can play with sums of money that you technically can't afford to lose, or at least couldn't if that money was not a part of your poker bankroll. For example, let's say you have an average job earning $40,000 per year. More than likely, you don't have much money to throw around in your everyday life. However, if you have a poker bankroll of $6,000, you could lose $500 or even $1,000 in a session and be able to shrug it off as just one of those things. In fact, you would have to be prepared to lose sums as large as that playing poker, even though a loss of that amount of money in "real life" would be a huge blow.

Your bankroll acts as a shield that allows you to behave in optimal risk-neutral ways, with sums of money that you would never risk losing away from the table. Keeping your poker bankroll completely independent is like having a second existence. You can be running badly at poker but still be perfectly well off in real life, and vice versa. You can have $20,000 in your poker bankroll and lose $1,000 at the turn of a card, yet still live a modest lifestyle saving quarters in a jar at home. A strong independent bankroll is the key to your poker freedom.

5. It can reassure those who don't understand poker.

Even in this day and age when poker is very much in the mainstream, most of the general public does not really understand the game, particularly in respect to how it is played by a serious player. If a tourist watches a $100-$200 limit game in Vegas, he sees players tossing $100 chips around as if they were nickels and thousands of dollars moving across the table at the turn of a card. He doesn't realize that the reason the players are so blasé about this kind of money is because they have six-digit bankrolls, and losing $1,000 on a hand simply isn't significant to them.

A lot of people are against all kinds of gambling, and poker is not an exception. In fact, poker is often seen as the worst kind of gambling because it conjures images of dark smoky rooms, shady characters, and innocent people being swindled out of their house and car. If you tell someone you play poker, and that person disapproves for religious or moral reasons, or has had the experience of seeing a life destroyed by gambling, then there is usually very little you can do to change his mind.

On the other hand, if someone is merely worried about you losing a lot of money because of a misconception, then you can reassure him by explaining your bankroll. The idea that you have a large financial cushion, which theoretically you should never lose, can be reassuring for someone uninformed about how the game works. If you are young and still under the sway of your parents, a bankroll might be the difference between you being able to play and not. At the very least, it might allow some members of your family to sleep better at night.

Of course, just because you have an independent bankroll doesn't mean there should never be any interaction between your bankroll and your checking account. As we stated in chapter 7, it is fine to cash out some of your winnings if you have a proper plan to do so or urgently need the money. The important thing is that the boundary between the two is clear. You don't dip into your bankroll as a matter of course; neither do you plow money into it. Keep the two worlds separate.

Obviously, if you are a professional player, then this is a different situation, as your poker bankroll is also your primary source of income. If this is the case, then you should have a plan for withdrawing from your bankroll. But it should be just that — a plan — not a haphazard integration of your poker bankroll with your day-to-day finances.

10.4. Emotional Separation

While bankroll separation is something that you just decide to do, maintaining emotional separation is extremely difficult and something you may never completely master. When we talk about emotional separation, we are really talking about two things:

1. Not bringing your real-life problems to the poker table and allowing them to affect your decisions.
2. Not allowing what happens at the poker table to spill over into the rest of your life.

Let's look at these in a little more detail.

Bringing real life to the table

The only thing on your mind when you play poker should be poker. Any other baggage that you bring to the table can only contribute to making bad decisions. Back in chapter 6, we discussed the best times to play poker, and one thing that we stressed was that you shouldn't have anything else preying on your mind.

If you are thinking about something excessively while away from the table, you are probably going to think about it excessively while at the table, too. It could be anything from a problem at work, to an argument you have just had, to a family problem, to a member of the opposite sex you can't get out of your mind.

Like most "problems" in poker, the solution is deceptively simple. If you have something on your mind that is dominating your thoughts at the expense of all else, then don't play poker. Of course, your brain will come up with all kinds of convoluted excuses why you should play, which will mostly be the same reasons it uses to convince you to continue to play when you know you are on tilt. You have to be firm and decide that you will play when in the best possible mental state or not at all.

The alternative is trying to play while not properly focused, which can put you in trouble from the start. At best, you are probably just not concentrating on the game properly and making sub-optimal decisions as a result. At worst, you could be heavily tilting under a wave of emotion that could lose you a lot of money.

In the former case, formulaic tilt is your biggest enemy, as you will not be considering all possible variables. In the latter case, you are prone to various types of tilt depending on your mood. If you are depressed, then passive tilt is usually the enemy, whereas if you are angry, then loose or aggressive tilt may influence your game. See chapter 6 for a full synopsis of the various types of tilt and what causes them.

Allowing poker to impinge upon the rest of your life

Determining when the game ends and real life begins can be a difficult problem to solve for the dedicated poker player. The difficulty is that you can't simply leave the poker table and forget about the game until you next sit down, because there are certain things you need to do away from the table. You will want to study your results, read poker literature, and think hard about how you can improve your game. Without doing these things, you are almost destined to fail.[74]

However, this is not when problems occur. The real thing you want to avoid is when the emotional fallout from a poker session starts to affect you away from the table. Sometimes poker players have problems preventing the emotions they experience at the poker table from carrying over, long after they have finished playing.

The most common manifestations are moods relating to how a session went. If we have a bad session, then we will be miserable for the rest of the day; if our session went well, we will be happy. Incidentally, this phenomenon is not unique to poker players. The same pattern is observed with avid sports fans when they see their team win or lose.

---

[74] Although, as discussed earlier in the chapter, you need to set limits on how much of your free time you spend doing this, lest you end up with no diversity in your life.

All players experience this to a certain extent. No matter how much we emphasize the long term or stress that individual sessions are not important, we will still feel happy after winning money and disappointed, angry, or depressed after losing it. The magnitude of these emotions will be directly related to how much we won or lost. As discussed in chapter 4, only a few players ever reach the stage where they are completely indifferent to short-term results.

If you are not one of these elite few, then your first goal is to minimize how bad sessions affect you personally.[75] Poker is no fun if it is going to put you in a bad mood afterwards. Try to put each bad session in perspective with your overall results. Convince yourself that you are destined to have bad sessions no matter how good a player you are. Try to look forward to the next session rather than back at the last one. Even after a complete train wreck of a session, you can normally take something positive from it; see how you can apply any lessons you have learned from that session.

Second, you might be feeling bad, but don't take it out on other people. Losing sessions are rarely anyone's fault (except sometimes your own), and they are certainly not the fault of your partner, family, children, or friends. They probably neither know nor understand the pain that poker players can suffer at the table. Don't persist in telling them bad beat stories or how unlucky you are, because, quite frankly, they are probably not interested even if they pretend to be. All it will do is foster a resentment of the effect poker has on you and hence of the game itself.

To fully incorporate poker into your life, make sure that the people important to you don't feel as if their own happiness is somehow related to your performance at the table.

If your spouse, partner, or kids worry about how your session is going, you have a bigger problem than worrying about bad beats. Try to be upbeat around others after a bad session. This doesn't have to be put on; tell yourself that you had a bad time at the table, which makes it

---

[75] Really, it is only the bad sessions we are worried about.

all the nicer to be away from it and in the company of other people. If someone asks how your session went, say something like "It didn't go too well, but that's poker" or "I lost today, but you have to take the ups with the downs." Reassure those around you that you are happy playing poker, and they will feel happier about the fact that you play.

> Action Point: If you have a spouse or partner who is affected in some way by the money you win or lose playing poker, sit down with him or her and plan how you will communicate your results. Although you might be able to separate your emotions from an individual session, your partner might not be. A good agreement might entail discussing your results once a month. This way, your partner can keep track of your results without having to live with the day-to-day fluctuations.

In summary, you really want to keep your poker life and the rest of your life as separate as possible. The trials and problems of everyday life will only hinder you at the poker table, while the emotions and the ups and downs of poker should not be allowed to interfere with the rest of your life. They are two separate worlds, and success at one could easily come at the expense of the other.

10.5. What Can You Learn from Poker?

Keeping your poker life and your real life as separate as possible doesn't mean that you can't take what you learn in one and apply it in the other. Naturally, when you started playing poker, you applied your worldly knowledge to the poker tables, especially when it came to things such as math, deductive reasoning, and judging character. In fact, we had to devote the whole of chapter 3 to explaining why in some situations you *can't* apply what you know in real life to the poker table.

What about the other way around? Can we take what we learn at the poker table and apply it to real life? In many cases, yes, we can. Some of the important lessons we learn at the poker table are very relevant in real-life situations. In effect, poker is a harsher, crueler version of the real world, where there are none of the soft landings that society usually gives us. Every sub-optimal decision, every mistake, every piece of woolly thinking, and every fundamental misunderstanding costs us money at the poker table. It's like starting a job where every time you make a mistake, even on your first day, money is taken out of your wages.

And those mistakes and misunderstandings are always your own fault. You can't lie about them, because you would only be lying to yourself. You can't blame the other guy, because the other guy doesn't care; he is busy stacking your chips. You can complain that it isn't fair, but it won't make a difference because poker doesn't pretend to be fair. If the worst happens and you manage to lose your whole bankroll, there is nobody to catch you, spot you a buy-in, and put you back in the game — at least, not usually.

As a result, many seasoned poker players tend to have a very focused view of the world, with much of the illusion that surrounds it removed. Effectively, playing good poker demands a certain way of tackling problems that you would be well advised to adopt in the rest of your life. Some commonly cited examples are:

- Using risk/reward analysis to analyze complex problems
- Eliminating irrelevant variables
- Choosing your opportunities carefully
- Exploiting an edge aggressively when one has been identified
- Taking full responsibility for your own life

The examples are many, especially if you are prepared to apply a bit of abstract thought. In fact, the entire Poker Mindset outlined in chapter 2 can be slightly rewritten to provide a pretty good mindset for life. Let's see what it reveals.

Understand and accept the realities of people and the world.

Understand the world that you live in. Never allow your curiosity for how things work to be satiated. Try to understand how people think and why they act the way they do, to better relate to and understand them. Never allow yourself to slip into a fantasy world where you see something or someone as how you would like it to be rather than how it actually is.

Live for the long term.

Make decisions based on what will make you happiest in the long term, not what will placate your immediate desires. Make plans and then work out the best way to achieve them. Don't get upset when something doesn't go your way in the short term, because things *will* go wrong in the short term and there is nothing you can do about it. Be satisfied that in the long term you will reap what you sow.

Concentrate on making the right decisions over getting the right results.

Overcome the crippling human tendency to judge a decision by its results and not on its merits. If you make a wise decision that doesn't work out for you, don't be afraid to make a similar decision again if the circumstances warrant it. Likewise, never assume a decision was correct just because it worked out well for you this time. Make enough right decisions, and the long-term results will take care of themselves.

Don't be scared of calculated risk.

In any situation, look at what is at stake and the potential reward, and calculate whether the latter is worth the former. Never "play scared" and overstate to yourself the significance of what you stand to lose. Be prepared to take good risks if doing so is beneficial to you in the long term. Never sit on your laurels with the attitude that says, "Better the devil you know than the devil you don't."

Leave your ego at home.

Never let your ego be a factor when making an important decision. Try to look objectively at what is best for you in real terms rather than what will satisfy your primal emotional need to feel good. When you are in a negotiation, always choose the option of getting the right result by looking weak rather than the wrong result by looking strong. Never allow a grudge to cloud your judgment or dictate your actions.

Act on logic rather than emotion.

Always think before you act; never let emotions (especially powerful ones) make decisions for you. How often have you had a fixed opinion on an issue only to change your mind overnight? After a night's sleep, all the short-term emotional factors evaporate, leaving you with cool-headed reasoning. If everyone else is telling you that you are acting irrationally, then consider the possibility that your emotions are clouding your judgment.

Dedicate yourself to a continuous cycle of self-improvement.

Be the best you can be. Decide on your goals in life and then work toward them. No matter how well you think you are doing, always have an area of your life that you are looking to improve. Climb to the very top of the mountain, and once you get there, start looking to the stars.

Seek to improve the other areas of your life the same way you would go about improving your poker game. Too many people neglect the former while concentrating on the latter. Hopefully, the Poker Mindset will help you master your emotions at the poker table to achieve better long-term results. At the same time, remember that poker can be a positive influence on the rest of your life if you just allow yourself to learn what it teaches you.

10.6. Chapter Review

❑ 10.1. The Missing Component of the Poker Mindset

- The missing component of the Poker Mindset is this: *Remember, poker is just a game.*
- The first seven attitudes of the Poker Mindset focused on maximizing your winnings at the poker table. Now with this missing component you can achieve true success.
- While the Poker Mindset says you need to "Remove All Emotion from Decisions," that doesn't mean you should necessarily remove all emotions from your game full stop. This is what we call the emotional paradox of poker.

❑ 10.2. Life Beyond the Poker Table

- Although you may spend a lot of time at the table, the important thing is not to do so at the expense of the rest of your life.
- Remember there is more to life than poker. You don't need to be playing, studying, or thinking about the game every free hour you have in order to be successful.

❑ 10.3. Bankroll Separation

- There are five distinct reasons that you should keep your poker bankroll completely separate from the rest of your day-to-day finances:
  1. It enables good bankroll management.
  2. You know how much you're winning or losing.
  3. It lessens the pressure to win.
  4. It allows you to play with large sums of money.
  5. It can reassure those who don't understand poker.

❑ 10.4. Emotional Separation

- When we talk about emotional separation, we are really talking about two things:
  1. Not bringing your real-life problems to the poker table and allowing them to affect your decisions.
  2. Not allowing what happens at the poker table to spill over into the rest of your life.
- To fully incorporate poker into your life, make sure that the people important to you don't feel as if their own happiness is somehow related to your performance at the table.

❑ 10.5. What Can You Learn from Poker?

- Keeping your poker life and your real life as separate as possible doesn't mean that you can't take what you learn in one and apply it in the other.
- Playing good poker demands a certain way of tackling problems that you would be well advised to adopt in the rest of your life. Some commonly cited examples are:
  - Using risk/reward analysis to analyze complex problems
  - Eliminating irrelevant variables
  - Choosing your opportunities carefully
  - Exploiting an edge aggressively when one has been identified
  - Taking full responsibility for your own life.
- The entire Poker Mindset outlined in chapter 2 can be slightly rewritten to provide a pretty good mindset for life.

276 **The Poker Mindset: Essential Attitudes for Poker Success**